MARY BERRY'S

Traditional puddings & desserts

MARY BERRY'S
Traditional puddings & desserts

Gorgeous classic recipes to treat family and friends

LONDON, NEW YORK, MELBOURNE,
MUNICH AND DELHI

Editor ANDREW ROFF
Designer KATHRYN WILDING
Managing editor DAWN HENDERSON
Managing art editor CHRISTINE KEILTY
Senior jacket creative NICOLA POWLING
Senior production editor JENNIFER MURRAY
Production controller BETHAN BLASE
Art director PETER LUFF
Publisher MARY-CLARE JERRAM

Photography EDWARD ALLWRIGHT AND WILLIAM REAVELL

DORLING KINDERSLEY (INDIA)
Editor SALONI TALWAR
Designer NEHA AHUJA
Art Director SHEFALI UPADHYAY
DTP designer TARUN SHARMA
DTP co-ordinator BALWANT SINGH
Head of publishing APARNA SHARMA

Material first published in *Mary Berry's Complete Cookbook* in 1995
This paperback edition published in Great Britain in 2011
by Dorling Kindersley Limited
80 Strand, London, WC2R 0RL

A Penguin Company

2 4 6 8 10 9 7 5 3 1

001–TD417–Jul/11

A CIP catalogue record for this book is available
from the British Library.

ISBN 978-1-4053-7348-7

Printed in
China by Leo

See our complete catalogue at
www.dk.com

CONTENTS

INTRODUCTION

I have so enjoyed putting together this collection. It only takes a few moments leafing through the following pages to realize that there really is a dessert for everyone and every occasion.

For me, a good dessert is the ultimate luxury, something so tempting you find yourself ordering it in a restaurant at every possible opportunity. What I have aimed to do is fill this book with my all-time favourite puddings and desserts that are just that: irresistible.

At the beginning you'll find a recipe choosers section, which makes light work of selecting a dessert. It showcases those that meet your particular needs, whatever they may be – from a craving of something chocolatey to a decadent treat that will impress your guests.

My first recipes are a range of classic pies, tarts, and crumbles, featuring such favourites as Lemon Meringue Pie and Bakewell Tart. Once you master pastry making, you'll realize just how easy these are to make. Double Crust Apple Pie guarantees to delight everyone in the family. Here, I've offered some variations that give this favourite a modern twist.

In winter the perfect dessert is something hot and hearty, something indulgent to cheer up the family. This is when my Hot Puddings chapter, next, will come in handy. You'll be surprised at how easy some of these puddings, such as Steamed Orange and Treacle Pudding, are to make. Others, such as Baklava, require a more delicate touch but the extra effort is well worth it.

Next comes the Chilled and Fruity Desserts chapter. Fresh fruit's clean crisp taste has a natural affinity with sugar, and will always provide you with something that looks stunning. Melt-in-your-mouth fruit cheesecakes and tangy fruit soufflés make for a fresher, lighter way to end a meal.

Full of flavour and smooth in texture, my selection of chilled and creamy desserts includes such classics as Crème Brûlée and Old English Trifle, as well as continental favourites such as Zabaglione and Tiramisu. A cold dessert contrasts with a hot main course, so it is always refreshing; make these desserts in advance and chill in the fridge until you're ready for them.

Lastly the Dessert Cakes chapter offers a range of home-baked cakes – ideal for eating at the coffee table or on the sofa, when meals are more informal with close family and friends. Best-ever Brownies and Coffee Éclairs make a great, indulgent after-dinner treat.

Presented with clear instructions that take you through each stage and with a beautiful photograph of the dessert, each recipe guarantees success. Dotted throughout the book, Key Techniques – such as how to make pastry and how to ice cakes using a piping bag – show you how to perfect your dessert-making skills so you will create something gorgeous every time.

I hope this selection of my favourite desserts will become yours too, and the whole family will continue to find them irresistible for years to come.

CHOCOLATE DESSERTS

Magic Chocolate Pudding *page 96*

Chocolate Cup Cakes *page 248*

Chocolate Delice *page 168*

Heavenly Chocolate Cake *page 214*

Chocolate-rum Mousse *page 170*

Devil's Food Cake *page 220*

Chocolate and Orange Mousse Cake *page 224*

Chocolate Terrine *page 192*

White Chocolate Gâteau *page 228*

Best-ever Brownies *page 246*

Chocolate Roulade *page 164*

Chocolate Profiteroles *page 234*

FRUIT DESSERTS

Raspberry Passion *page 130*

Raspberry Meringue Roulade *page 204*

Apple Brown Betty *page 76*

Tropical Fruit Cheesecake *page 116*

Double Crust Apple Pie *page 64*

Tropical Tartlets *page 60*

French Apple Tart *page 48*

Strawberry and Rhubarb Pie *page 68*

Jamaican Bananas *page 104*

Tropical Fruit Salad *page 148*

Cherry Cheesecake *page 132*

Marbled Raspberry Cheescake *page 138*

Mid-summer Pudding *page 142*

Apple Charlotte *page 90*

Tarte Tatin *page 26*

OUT TO IMPRESS

Tarte Tatin *page 26*

Apple Tarte au Citron *page 38*

Mille-feuille *page 44*

French Apple Tart *page 48*

Pecan Pie *page 50*

Mincemeat and Almond Tart *page 56*

Tart au Citron *page 58*

Raspberry Meringue Roulade *page 204*

Baklava *page 94*

Tropical Fruit Cheesecake *page 116*

Chilled Lemon Soufflé *page 120*

Cherry Cheesecake *page 132*

Marbled Raspberry Cheesecake *page 138*

White Chocolate Gâteau *page 228*

Hazelnut Meringue Gâteau *page 182*

Chocolate Terrine *page 192*

Tropical Tartlets *page 60*

Divine Tiramisu *page 200*

Stem Ginger and Pineapple Pavlova *page 206*

Baked Alaska *page 196*

PREPARE AHEAD

Bakewell Tart *page 32*

Mille-feuille *page 44*

Mincemeat and Almond Tart *page 56*

Rice Pudding *page 80*

Iced Lime Traybake *page 240*

Christmas Pudding *page 88*

Treacle Tart *page 34*

Chilled Lemon Soufflé *page 120*

Austrian Cheesecake *page 160*

Mid-summer Pudding *page 142*

Chocolate and Orange Mousse Cake *page 224*

Old English Trifle *page 154*

Chocolate Delice *page 168*

Tropical Fruit Cheesecake *page 116*

Divine Tiramisu *page 200*

Tropical Fruit Salad *page 148*

Luxury Crème Caramel *page 202*

KEEP IT SIMPLE

Apple Brown Betty *page 76*

Rice Pudding *page 80*

Magic Chocolate Pudding *page 96*

French Pancakes *page 98*

Lemon Sorbet *page 134*

Tropical Fruit Salad *page 148*

Gooseberry Fool *page 112*

Rich Vanilla Ice Cream *page 186*

Meringue Raspberry Nests *page 176*

Crème Brûlée *page 162*

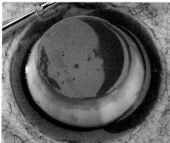

Luxury Crème Caramel *page 202*

Lemon Pannacotta *page 210*

Iced Lime Traybake *page 240*

INDULGENT DESSERTS

Pecan Pie *page 50*

Divine Tiramisu *page 200*

Magic Chocolate Pudding *page 96*

Treacle and Orange Pudding *page 108*

Chocolate Delice *page 168*

Chocolate Roulade *page 164*

Iced Christmas Pudding *page 198*

White Chocolate Gâteau *page 228*

Sticky Toffee Pudding *page 78*

Rich Vanilla Ice Cream *page 186*

Chocolate Profiteroles *page 234*

Chocolate Terrine *page 192*

Chocolate-rum Mousse *page 170*

Best-ever Brownies *page 246*

Devil's Food Cake *page 220*

Chocolate and Orange Mousse Cake *page 224*

Baklava *page 94*

Stem Ginger and Pineapple Pavlova *page 206*

Hazelnut Meringue Gâteau *page 182*

DESSERTS FOR A CROWD

Tropical Fruit Cheesecake *page 116*

French Apple Tart *page 48*

Lemon Meringue Pie *page 52*

Mincemeat and Almond Tart *page 56*

Tarte au Citron *page 58*

Rice Pudding *page 80*

Hazelnut Meringue Gâteau *page 182*

Mille-feuille *page 44*

Old English Trifle *page 154*

Rich Bread and Butter Pudding *page 106*

Divine Tiramisu *page 200*

Stem Ginger and Pineapple Pavlova *page 206*

Heavenly Chocolate Cake *page 214*

Chocolate and Orange Mousse Cake *page 224*

White Chocolate Gâteau *page 228*

Banoffi Pie *page 36*

Apple Tart au Citron *page 38*

Marbled Coffee Ring Cake *page 242*

Pies, Tarts, and Crumbles

TARTE TATIN

SERVES 6

SHALLOW 23CM (9IN) ROUND CAKE TIN

90g (3oz) butter
90g (3oz) demerara sugar
1kg (2lb) Cox's apples or similar
   firm eating apples
grated zest and juice of 1 lemon

PASTRY

175g (6oz) plain flour
125g (4oz) chilled butter, cubed
30g (1oz) icing sugar
1 egg yolk
about 1 tbsp cold water

1 Make the pastry: put the flour into a large bowl and add the butter. Rub in until the mixture resembles fine breadcrumbs. Stir in the icing sugar, then mix in the egg yolk and enough water to make a soft, but not sticky, dough. Wrap and chill in the refrigerator for 30 minutes.

2 Put the butter and sugar into a pan and heat gently until the sugar dissolves. Increase the heat and cook gently for 4–5 minutes until the mixture turns dark golden brown and is thick, but pourable. Pour evenly over the bottom of the tin. (Do not use a loose-bottomed or springform tin, as the caramel will leak.)

3 Peel, core, and slice the apples. Toss them with the lemon zest and juice. Arrange a single layer of the best apple slices in a circular pattern on top of the caramel mixture. Cover evenly with the remaining apple slices.

4 Roll out the pastry on a lightly floured surface into a round slightly larger than the tin. Lay the pastry over the apples, tucking the excess down the side of the tin.

5 Bake in a preheated oven at 200°C (400°F, Gas 6) for 25–30 minutes until the pastry is crisp and golden brown. Invert a serving plate on top of the tin, turn the tin and plate over, and lift the tin to reveal the caramelized apples. Serve warm or cold with cream.

KEY TECHNIQUES

SHORTCRUST PASTRY

A blend of 2 parts flour, 1 part fat, and usually water, shortcrust pastry is used for sweet and savoury pies and tarts. Chill the pastry for the time given in the recipe to stop it shrinking when in the oven. Use shortcrust pastry to make Treacle Tart (page 34), and Strawberry and Rhubard Pie (page 68). These quantities make sufficient pastry to line a 23–25cm (9–10in) flan dish, flan tin, or pie dish.

1 Sift 175g (6oz) plain flour into a bowl. Cut 90g (3oz) well-chilled butter or lard into small pieces and add to the bowl. Stir to coat the fat with flour. If using a food processor, pulse the flour with the fat until like breadcrumbs.

2 Quickly and lightly rub the fat into the flour, lifting the mixture to incorporate air, until like fine breadcrumbs. Sprinkle over 2 tbsp cold water and stir gently with a table knife to mix. Add a little more water if the pastry seems too dry.

3 Gather the mixture together and knead briefly until smooth (handle the dough as little as possible or the pastry will be tough). If the dough is sticky, add a little more flour. Shape into a ball, wrap, and chill for 30 minutes. In the food processor, add the water, pulse briefy, turn out onto a floured surface, and knead lightly to make a smooth dough.

PÂTE SUCRÉE

Bound with egg yolks, pâte sucrée is richer than shortcrust pastry and is used for sweet tarts and tartlets. The classic method for mixing the dough is on a flat marble work surface. These quantities make sufficient pastry to line a 25cm (10in) flan dish, tin, or pie dish.

1 Sift 200g (7oz) plain flour on to a work surface. Make a well in the middle and add 90g (3oz) softened butter, 60g (2oz) caster sugar, and 3 egg yolks. With your fingertips blend together the butter, sugar, and egg yolks.

2 Using your fingertips, gradually work the sifted flour into the blended butter mixture until the mixture resembles coarse crumbs and all the butter has disappeared. If the mixture seems too sticky, work in a little more flour.

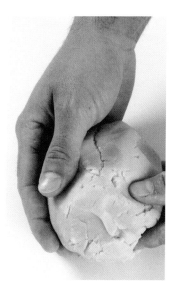

3 With your fingers or a pastry scraper, gather the dough into a ball, then knead briefly until it is smooth and pliable. Shape the dough into a ball again, wrap, and chill for 30 minutes or until it feels just firm.

KEY TECHNIQUES

QUICK PUFF PASTRY

This light, crispy pastry is made by rolling and folding the dough many times to make paper-thin layers. When making quick puff pastry, unlike puff pastry, the butter is added all at the same time, in large cubes. For many dishes, quick puff pastry can be used instead of puff pastry. Use this technique when making Double Crust Apple Pie (page 64). These quantities make sufficient pastry for a 25cm (10in) double-crust pie.

1 Sift 250g (8oz) plain flour into a bowl. Add 90g (3oz) each of chilled cubed butter and white vegetable fat, and stir to coat in flour. Add about 150ml (¼ pint) cold water into the bowl and, with a table knife, bind to a lumpy dough.

2 Roll out the dough into a rectangle 3 times as long as it is wide. Fold the bottom third up and the top third down. Press the edges to seal. Wrap and chill for 15 minutes, then place so the folded edges are to the sides.

3 Roll out the dough into a rectangle and fold as before. Turn the dough so the folded edges are to the sides again. Repeat the rolling, folding, and turning twice more. Wrap and chill for 30 minutes.

OTHER TYPES OF PASTRY

Puff pastry
Like quick-puff and flaky pastry, this is rolled and folded. Ready-made fresh or frozen puff pastry is very convenient, but not all brands are made with butter. Puff pastry is often used as a top crust for sweet and savoury pies, to wrap beef Wellington, and for Mille-feuille (page 44.)

Flaky pastry
This is a short-cut version of puff pastry. The rolling and folding process is repeated only a few times. It is used for pies and tarts.

Filo and strudel pastry
These are similar types of pastry made from a pliable dough that is stretched and rolled until extremely thin. It is then rolled around a filling or layered with melted butter. Filo and strudel pastries are difficult to make at home, but ready-made varieties are available fresh and frozen. Use filo pastry for making Baklava (page 94.)

SERVES 6

19CM (7½IN) LOOSE-BOTTOMED FLUTED FLAN TIN

125g (4oz) butter
125g (4oz) caster sugar
1 egg, lightly beaten
125g (4oz) cornflour or semolina
½ tsp almond extract
2 tbsp raspberry jam
icing sugar for sprinkling

PASTRY

175g (6oz) plain flour
45g (1½oz) chilled butter, cubed
45g (1½oz) chilled white vegetable
 fat, cubed
about 2 tbsp cold water
milk for glazing

BAKEWELL TART

1 Make the pastry: put the flour into a large bowl. Rub in the butter and vegetable fat until the mixture resembles fine breadcrumbs. Mix in enough water to make a soft, pliable dough. Roll out the pastry on a lightly floured work surface and use to line the flan tin. Reserve the trimmings for decorating the tart and chill the tart in the refrigerator for 30 minutes.

2 Melt the butter in a saucepan, stir in the caster sugar, and cook for about 1 minute. Remove from the heat, leave to cool a little, then gradually stir in the egg, cornflour or semolina, and almond extract.

3 Spread the jam evenly over the bottom of the pastry case, and pour the almond mixture on top.

4 Roll out the reserved pastry trimmings, and cut into strips that will fit across the tart. Arrange the strips on top of the almond filling to form a lattice, attaching them to the pastry case with a little milk.

5 Bake on a hot baking tray in a preheated oven at 200°C (400°F, Gas 6) for 45–50 minutes until the filling is well risen and golden and springs back when lightly pressed with a finger. If the pastry is browning too much, cover the tart loosely with foil.

6 Remove the tart from the oven. Sprinkle with icing sugar and serve the tart warm or cold.

TREACLE TART

SERVES 8

25CM (10IN) LOOSE-BOTTOMED FLUTED FLAN TIN

375g (12oz) golden syrup
about 200g (7oz) fresh white
   or brown breadcrumbs
grated zest and juice of 1 large lemon

PASTRY

175g (6oz) plain flour
90g (3oz) chilled butter, cubed
about 2 tbsp cold water

1 Make the pastry: put the flour into a large bowl, add the butter, and rub in with the fingertips until the mixture resembles fine breadcrumbs. Mix in enough water to make a soft pliable dough.

2 Roll out the dough on a lightly floured surface and use to line the flan tin. Chill in the refrigerator for 30 minutes.

3 Gently heat the golden syrup in a saucepan until melted, and stir in the breadcrumbs and lemon zest and juice. Pour into the pastry case.

4 Bake on a hot baking tray in a preheated oven at 200°C (400°F, Gas 6) for 10 minutes; reduce the oven temperature to 180°C (350°F, Gas 4), and bake for a further 30 minutes or until the pastry is golden and the filling firm.

5 Leave to cool in the tin for a few minutes. Serve warm, cut into slices.

BANOFFI PIE

SERVES 6

18CM (7IN) LOOSE-BOTTOMED FLUTED FLAN TIN

60g (2oz) butter

1 × 400g (13oz) can sweetened condensed milk

2 bananas, peeled and sliced

150ml (¼ pint) double cream, lightly whipped

30g (1oz) plain chocolate, grated, to decorate

BISCUIT CRUST

60g (2oz) butter

150g (5oz) ginger biscuits, crushed

1 Make the biscuit crust: melt the butter in a saucepan, add the crushed biscuits, and stir well to combine. Press on to the bottom and side of the flan tin. Chill until firm.

2 Melt the butter in a small saucepan over a low heat. Stir until the butter has melted.

3 Add the condensed milk to the pan, and heat gently, stirring constantly, until the mixture is a pale caramel colour, about 10 minutes. The butter may separate from the condensed milk, but the mixture will be smooth when cooled slightly.

4 Pour the mixture into the biscuit crust and leave to cool. Chill until the caramel filling is set.

5 Arrange the banana slices evenly over the caramel filling. Top with the whipped cream, and decorate with the grated chocolate. Serve chilled.

SERVES 10

DEEP 25CM (10IN) LOOSE-BOTTOMED FLAN TIN

4 eggs
250g (8oz) caster sugar
finely grated zest and juice of 2 lemons
125g (4oz) butter, melted
2 large cooking apples, eg Bramley's,
   quartered, cored, and peeled – about
   350g (12oz) prepared weight
2 red eating apples, quartered, cored,
   and thinly sliced (leave the red skin on)
about 30g (1oz) demerara sugar

PASTRY

250g (8oz) plain flour
30g (1oz) icing sugar
125g (4oz) butter, cubed
1 egg, beaten
1 tbsp water

APPLE TARTE AU CITRON

1 Make the pastry: sift the flour and icing sugar into a bowl and rub in the cubes of butter until the mixture resembles breadcrumbs. Stir in the egg and water and bring together to form a dough.

2 Roll out the dough on a lightly floured surface and use to line the flan tin. Chill in the refrigerator for about 30 minutes.

3 Prepare the filling: beat the eggs, caster sugar, and lemon zest and juice in a bowl. Stir in the warm melted butter, then coarsely grate the cooking apples directly into the mixture and mix well.

4 Spread the runny lemon mixture in the chilled pastry case. Level the surface with the back of a spoon and arrange the red-skinned apples around the outside edge.

5 Bake on a hot baking tray in a preheated oven at 200°C (400°F, Gas 6) for about 40–50 minutes or until the centre feels firm to the touch and the apples are tinged brown and pastry crisp. Serve warm or cold with cream.

clockwise from top left: *Blackberry and Apple Cobbler, Classic Apple Crumble, and Apple Tarte au Citron*

CLASSIC APPLE CRUMBLE

SERVES 6

SHALLOW 20CM (8IN) OVENPROOF DISH

900g (2lb) cooking apples, eg Bramley's
175g (6oz) granulated sugar
finely grated zest of 1 lemon
6 tbsp water

TOPPING

175g (6oz) plain flour
90g (3oz) butter
60g (2oz) demerara sugar

1 Quarter, peel, and core the apples, then slice them fairly thinly. Toss the slices in the sugar, lemon zest, and water. Put in the ovenproof dish.

2 Make the topping: put the flour in a bowl and rub in the butter until the mixture resembles fine breadcrumbs, then stir in the sugar.

3 Sprinkle the topping evenly over the apple mixture in the dish and bake in a preheated oven at 180°C (350°F, Gas 4) for 40–45 minutes until golden brown and bubbling.

Illustrated on page 39.

Cook's know-how

For a crunchier topping on the Classic Apple Crumble, use 125g (4oz) wholemeal flour and 60g (2oz) porridge oats or muesli instead of the plain flour.
To sweeten cooking apples, especially windfall apples that are not at their best, use apricot jam instead of some – or all – of the sugar. Apricot jam gives a gentle sweetness, and it improves the texture of the apples, especially if you are using them for a purée or a pie.

Apples have a natural affinity with pastry and they are the best of fruits to cook with.

SERVES 4

5CM (2IN) ROUND FLUTED BISCUIT CUTTER

2 cooking apples, eg Bramley's
500g (1lb) blackberries
60g (2oz) caster sugar
finely grated zest and juice of 1 lemon

COBBLER TOPPING

250g (8oz) self-raising flour
60g (2oz) butter, cubed
90g (3oz) caster sugar
90ml (3fl oz) milk, plus extra for glazing

BLACKBERRY AND APPLE COBBLER

1 Quarter, peel, and core the apples, then cut into large slices, about 1cm (½in) thick.

2 Put the apples into a saucepan with the blackberries, sugar, and lemon zest and juice. Cover and simmer gently for 10–15 minutes until the apple pieces are tender but not broken up.

3 Meanwhile, make the cobbler topping: put the flour into a bowl, add the cubes of butter, and rub in with the fingertips until the mixture resembles fine breadcrumbs. Stir in the sugar, add the milk, and mix to form a soft dough.

4 Roll out the dough on a lightly floured surface until 1cm (½in) thick. Cut out as many shapes as you can with the biscuit cutter. If you do not have a biscuit cutter, stamp out rounds with the rim of a glass or coffee mug.

5 Transfer the fruit to an ovenproof dish, arrange the pastry shapes on top, and brush with milk to glaze.

6 Bake in a preheated oven at 220°C (425°F, Gas 7) for 15–20 minutes until the topping is golden.

Illustrated on page 39.

The rich, tart taste of fresh blackberries contrasts well with the sweet taste of cooked apples.

MILLE-FEUILLE

SERVES 6

250g (8oz) puff pastry, thawed if frozen
3 tbsp raspberry jam
150ml (¼ pint) double or
   whipping cream, whipped

CRÈME PÂTISSIÈRE

2 eggs, beaten
60g (2oz) caster sugar
30g (1oz) plain flour
300ml (½ pint) milk
½ tsp vanilla extract

ICING

125g (4oz) icing sugar
about 1 tbsp water

1 Make the crème pâtissière (page 233), using the quantities listed left.

2 Roll out the pastry on a floured surface to make a thin, 28 × 33cm (11 × 13in) rectangle. Lay it over a dampened baking tray. Prick the pastry with a fork. Bake in a preheated oven at 220°C (425°F, Gas 7) for 10–15 minutes until the pastry is crisp and a pale golden brown colour.

3 Remove from the oven and leave to cool. Reduce the oven temperature to 180°C (350°F, Gas 4). Trim the edges of the pastry to a rectangle, then cut into 3 equal rectangles, 10cm (4in) wide. Crush the pastry trimmings and set aside.

4 Mix the icing sugar and enough water to make a smooth glacé icing. Spread over 1 of the rectangles, and place on a baking tray. Bake for 2 minutes or until the icing has just set and has a slight sheen. Leave to cool.

5 Place a second pastry rectangle on a serving plate. Spread evenly with the jam and then the whipped cream. Set the third rectangle on top and cover with the crème pâtissière.

6 Top with the iced pastry rectangle. Decorate the long edges of the rectangle with thin rows of crushed pastry trimmings. Chill the mille-feuille in the refrigerator until ready to serve.

KEY TECHNIQUES

MAKING A PASTRY CASE

Careful handling of pastry dough should ensure it does not shrink or distort when baking. Use this technique when making Bakewell Tart (page 32), Treacle Tart (page 34), Apple Tart au Citron (page 38), French Apple Tart (page 48), Pecan Pie (page 50), Lemon Meringue Pie (page 52), Mincemeat and Almond Tart (page 56), Tarte au Citron (page 58), Double Crust Apple Pie (page 64), and Strawberry and Rhubarb Pie (page 68).

1 Put the pastry dough on a floured work surface and flour the rolling pin to stop the pastry sticking. Roll out into a round, starting in the middle each time and lifting and turning the pastry round a quarter turn after each roll.

2 If lining a pie dish, roll out the pastry dough to a round 5cm (2in) larger than the top of the dish; a pastry lid should also be 5cm (2in) larger. Roll the pastry up loosely around the rolling pin, and unroll over the edges of the dish.

3 Gently ease the pastry into the dish, pressing it firmly and neatly into the bottom edge. Be very careful not to stretch the pastry. Carefully trim off the excess pastry with a table knife. If there are any holes, patch them with the trimmings of pastry dough.

1 Prick the pastry case all over with a fork. Line with foil or greaseproof paper, allowing it to come above the rim so the baked tart will lift out easily.

2 Fill the case with ceramic baking beans, dried pulses, or uncooked rice, and bake in a preheated oven at 190°C (375°F, Gas 5) for 10 minutes.

3 Remove the beans and foil. Return the case to the oven and bake for 5 minutes (part-baked) or 15 minutes (fully baked). If the pastry rises during baking, gently press it down with your hand.

FRENCH APPLE TART

SERVES 8–10

28CM (11IN) LOOSE-BOTTOMED FLUTED FLAN TIN
BAKING BEANS

90g (3oz) butter
1.5kg (3lb) cooking apples, quartered,
   cored, and cut into chunks
3 tbsp water
6 tbsp apricot jam
125g (4oz) caster sugar
grated zest of 1 large lemon

APPLE TOPPING AND GLAZE

375g (12oz) eating apples, quartered,
   cored, peeled, and thinly sliced
juice of 1 lemon
1 tbsp caster sugar
6 tbsp apricot jam

PASTRY

250g (8oz) plain flour
125g (4oz) chilled butter, cubed
125g (4oz) caster sugar
4 egg yolks

1 Make the pastry: put the flour into a bowl and rub in the butter until the mixture resembles fine breadcrumbs. Stir in the sugar, then the egg yolks and a little cold water to make a soft dough. Roll out the pastry on a lightly floured surface and use to line the flan tin. Chill in the refrigerator for 30 minutes.

2 Melt the butter in a large saucepan, and add the cooking apples and water. Cover and cook very gently for 20–25 minutes until the apples are soft.

3 Rub the apples through a nylon sieve into a clean pan. Add the jam, sugar, and lemon zest. Cook over a high heat for 15–20 minutes, stirring constantly, until all the liquid has evaporated and the apple purée is thick. Leave to cool.

4 Bake the pastry case blind (page 47) in a preheated oven at 190°C (375°F, Gas 5) for 10–15 minutes. Remove the beans and foil and bake for another 5 minutes. Leave to cool.

5 Spoon the purée into the case. Arrange the apple slices on top, brush with lemon juice, and sprinkle with caster sugar. Bake for another 30–35 minutes until the apples are tender and their edges browned.

6 Heat the jam, work through a sieve, then brush over the apples. Serve warm or cold.

PECAN PIE

SERVES 6–8

23CM (9IN) LOOSE-BOTTOMED FLUTED FLAN TIN
BAKING BEANS

150g (5oz) pecan halves
30g (1oz) unsalted butter
60g (2oz) light muscovado sugar
30g (1oz) caster sugar
125ml (4fl oz) golden syrup
3 tbsp brandy
1 tsp vanilla extract
2 tbsp single cream
¼ tsp ground cinnamon
pinch of grated nutmeg
1 large egg, lightly beaten
2 egg yolks

PASTRY

175g (6oz) plain flour
90g (3oz) chilled butter, cubed
about 2 tbsp cold water
1 egg white, lightly beaten

1 Make the pastry: put the flour into a bowl, add the butter, and rub in with the fingertips until the mixture resembles fine breadcrumbs. Add enough water to make a soft dough. Roll out the pastry on a lightly floured work surface and line the flan tin. Chill in the refrigerator for 30 minutes.

2 Bake blind (page 47) in a preheated oven at 180°C (350°F, Gas 4) for 10 minutes. Remove the beans and foil, lightly brush the pastry case with egg white, and return to the oven for about another 5 minutes or until cooked.

3 Meanwhile, toast the pecans in a preheated oven at 180°C (350°F, Gas 4), turning occasionally, for 10–15 minutes. Reserve a few pecan halves and coarsely chop the remainder.

4 Put the butter into a heavy-based saucepan and cook over a gentle heat until golden brown. Add the sugars and golden syrup, and heat gently until the sugars dissolve. Add the brandy, bring to a boil, and cook for 5 minutes. Remove from the heat and stir in the vanilla extract, cream, cinnamon, and nutmeg.

5 Whisk together the egg and egg yolks. Whisk a little hot syrup into the eggs. Add half of the syrup, little by little, then add the remainder. Leave to cool.

6 Arrange the chopped pecans and pecan halves in the pastry case. Pour the syrup and egg mixture over them. Bake in a preheated oven at 180°C (350°F, Gas 4) for 40 minutes until golden and set. Serve cool.

LEMON MERINGUE PIE

SERVES 8–10

25CM (10IN) LOOSE-BOTTOMED FLUTED FLAN TIN
BAKING BEANS

grated zest and juice of 4 large lemons
90g (3oz) cornflour
600ml (1 pint) water
4 egg yolks
175g (6oz) caster sugar

MERINGUE

5 egg whites
250g (8oz) caster sugar

PASTRY

250g (8oz) plain flour
30g (1oz) icing sugar
125g (4oz) chilled butter, cubed
1 egg yolk
2 tbsp cold water

1 Make the pastry: sift the flour and icing sugar into a large bowl. Add the butter and rub in with the fingertips until the mixture resembles fine breadcrumbs. Mix in the egg yolk and enough cold water to make a soft, pliable dough. Roll out the dough on a lightly floured surface and use to line the flan tin. Chill in the refrigerator for 30 minutes.

2 Bake blind (page 47) in a preheated oven at 200°C (400°F, Gas 6) for 10 minutes.

3 Remove the baking beans and foil and bake the pastry case for 5 minutes or until the base has dried out. Remove from the oven and reduce the temperature to 150°C (300°F, Gas 2).

4 Mix the lemon zest and juice with the cornflour. Bring the water to a boil, then stir into the lemon mixture. Return to the pan and bring back to a boil, stirring, until the mixture thickens. Remove from heat.

5 Leave to cool slightly, then stir in the egg yolks and sugar. Return to a low heat and cook, stirring, until just simmering. Pour into the pastry case.

6 Whisk the egg whites until stiff but not dry. Whisk in the sugar, 1 tsp at a time, on full speed. Pile on top of the filling and spread over evenly. Bake for 45 minutes or until crisp and pale brown. Serve the pie warm or cold.

KEY TECHNIQUES

DECORATING WITH PASTRY

Pies and tarts

Keep pastry trimmings to make small decorative shapes. Cut them freehand or use cutters. They can be fixed to the edge of a pastry case or arranged on a lid. If the pastry has a glaze, attach the shapes with water, then apply the glaze all over the pie, brushing it on gently so the shapes are not disturbed.

A pastry lid can be brushed with a glaze before baking. A little milk or beaten egg will give a shiny finish, as will egg white alone – this is a good way to use up whites when the pastry is made with egg yolks. Sprinkle a pastry lid with sugar for a crisp, sweet glaze.

Decorative edges

A simple way to give a decorative finish to a pie is to crimp the edge. Place the tips of the thumb and forefinger of one hand against the outside rim of the dish. With the forefinger of your other hand, gently push the pastry edge outwards between the thumb and finger, and pinch the pastry to make a rounded "V" shape. Repeat this action all around the pastry lid. Alternatively, push and pinch in the opposite direction, working from the outside of the edge inwards to achieve a different pattern.

MICROWAVING PIES, TARTS, AND CRUMBLES

The microwave can be a helpful tool when preparing pies, tarts, and hot desserts. For baking pastry-based pies and tarts, however, there really is no substitute for the conventional oven.

The microwave is perfect for cooking fruit fillings for pies and tarts. The fruit remains plump and colourful. It can also be used to melt or soften butter and to heat liquids in which fruit is left to soak. Under careful watch, the microwave can be used to melt chocolate and to make caramel.

FREEZING PIES, TARTS, AND CRUMBLES

Crumbles freeze well both before and after cooking. Pastry dough is an excellent freezer standby; thaw before rolling out. Unbaked pastry cases are ideal for last-minute desserts as they can be baked from frozen. Baked pastries you can freeze include Treacle Tart (page 34), Mincemeat and Almond Tart (page 56), and Pecan Pie (page 50).

SERVES 8–10

DEEP 28CM (11IN) LOOSE-BOTTOMED FLUTED FLAN TIN

175g (6oz) butter, softened
175g (6oz) caster sugar
4 eggs
175g (6oz) ground almonds
1 tsp almond essence
about 8 tbsp good-quality mincemeat

PASTRY

250g (8oz) plain flour
125g (4oz) chilled butter, cubed
60g (2oz) caster sugar
1 egg, beaten
1 tbsp water

TOPPING

175g (6oz) icing sugar, sifted
juice of ½ lemon
1–2 tbsp water
60g (2oz) flaked almonds

MINCEMEAT AND ALMOND TART

1 Make the pastry: put the flour into a large bowl. Add the butter and rub in with the fingertips until the mixture resembles fine breadcrumbs. Stir in the sugar, then mix in the egg and water to bind to a soft, pliable dough. Roll out the dough on a lightly floured surface and use to line the tin. Prick the bottom with a fork. Cover and chill while preparing the filling.

2 Put the butter and sugar into a large bowl and cream together until pale and fluffy. Add the eggs one at a time, beating well after each addition, then mix in the ground almonds and almond essence.

3 Spread the mincemeat evenly over the bottom of the pastry case. Pour the almond mixture over the mincemeat.

4 Bake on a hot baking tray in a preheated oven at 190°C (375°F, Gas 5) for about 40 minutes until the filling is golden and firm to the touch. Cover loosely with foil if it is browning too much.

5 Meanwhile, make the topping: stir together the icing sugar, lemon juice, and enough water to make a thin glacé icing. Spread evenly over the tart, then sprinkle with the almonds. Return to the oven for 5 minutes or until the icing is shiny and the almonds lightly coloured. Serve warm or cold.

SERVES 10–12

28CM (11IN) LOOSE-BOTTOMED FLUTED FLAN TIN
BAKING BEANS

9 eggs
300ml (½ pint) double cream
grated zest and juice of 5 large lemons
375g (12oz) caster sugar
icing sugar for dusting
lemon twists to decorate

PASTRY

250g (8oz) plain flour
125g (4oz) chilled butter, cubed
60g (2oz) caster sugar
1 egg
1 tbsp water

TARTE AU CITRON

1 Make the pastry: put the flour into a large bowl. Add the butter and rub in with the fingertips until the mixture resembles fine breadcrumbs. Stir in the caster sugar, then bind together with the egg and water to make a soft, pliable dough.

2 Roll out the dough on a lightly floured surface and use to line the flan tin. Chill in the refrigerator for 30 minutes.

3 Meanwhile, beat the eggs in a bowl and add the cream, lemon zest and juice, and caster sugar. Stir until smooth.

4 Bake the pastry case blind (page 47) in a preheated oven at 200°C (400°F, Gas 6) for 10 minutes.

5 Remove the baking beans and foil and bake the pastry case for 5 minutes or until the base has dried out. Remove from the oven and reduce the temperature to 180°C (350°F, Gas 4).

6 Pour the lemon mixture into the pastry case.

7 Bake for 35–40 minutes until the lemon filling has set. Cover the tart loosely with foil if the pastry begins to brown too much.

8 Leave the tart to cool a little, then dust with icing sugar. Decorate with lemon twists, and serve warm or at room temperature.

TROPICAL TARTLETS

MAKES 10

10 × 7CM (3IN) ROUND TARTLET TINS OR
   BOAT-SHAPED TINS (BARQUETTE MOULDS)

about 600ml (1 pint) ready-made
   thick custard
1 × 200g (7oz) can mandarin oranges
   in natural juice, well drained
1 × 200g (7oz) can apricot halves
   in natural juice, well drained
   and cut into pieces
about 3 tbsp apricot jam
about 60g (2oz) toasted flaked almonds

ALMOND PASTRY

60g (2oz) ground almonds
125g (4oz) plain flour
2 tbsp caster sugar
90g (3oz) chilled butter, cubed
about 3 tbsp cold water

1 Make the pastry: combine the almonds, flour, and sugar in a bowl. Add the butter and rub in with the fingertips until the mixture resembles fine breadcrumbs. Add enough cold water to make a soft pliable dough.

2 Put the pastry on a floured surface and flatten slightly. Place a large sheet of baking parchment on top and roll out the pastry, beneath the parchment, until about 3mm (⅛in) thick. Line the tartlet tins with pastry and chill in the refrigerator for 15 minutes.

3 Prick the pastry all over and bake in a preheated oven at 190°C (375°F, Gas 5) for 12–15 minutes. Leave the cases to cool in the tins for 10 minutes. Remove and transfer to a wire rack. Leave to cool.

4 Spoon custard into each case, then top with the mandarin oranges and apricots. Melt the jam in a small pan, sieve, then spoon over the fruit. Sprinkle with the almonds and leave to set before serving.

RASPBERRY TARTLETS

MAKES 16

16 × 6CM (2½IN) ROUND TARTLET TINS
7CM (3IN) PASTRY CUTTER

250g (8oz) mascarpone
2 tbsp caster sugar
350g (12oz) raspberries
3 tbsp redcurrant jelly
1–2 tsp lemon juice to taste

PASTRY

250g (8oz) plain flour
125g (4oz) chilled butter, cubed
2 tbsp caster sugar
3–4 tbsp cold water

1 Make the pastry: put the flour into a bowl, add the butter, and rub in with the fingertips until the mixture resembles fine breadcrumbs. Stir in the sugar, then add enough cold water to the pastry to make a soft pliable dough.

2 On a lightly floured surface, roll out the pastry thinly. Using the pastry cutter, cut out 16 rounds. Gently press the rounds into the tartlet tins and chill in the refrigerator for 15 minutes.

3 Prick all over with a fork and bake blind (page 47) in a preheated oven at 190°C (375°F, Gas 5) for 12–15 minutes until golden. Leave in the tins for 10 minutes, then remove and transfer to a wire rack. Leave to cool completely.

4 Beat together the mascarpone and sugar and spoon into the pastry cases. Top with the raspberries, pressing them gently into the filling.

5 Melt the jelly with lemon juice to taste in a small pan, then spoon over the fruits. Leave to set before serving.

*Freshly picked raspberries look stunning on tarts.
Their tangy taste complements the creamy
texture of the filling too.*

DOUBLE CRUST APPLE PIE

SERVES 6

24CM (9½IN) PIE DISH

500g (1lb) cooking apples, preferably
 Bramley's, quartered, cored,
 peeled, and sliced
250g (8oz) Cox's apples, quartered,
 cored, peeled, and sliced
about 30g (1oz) caster sugar,
 plus extra for sprinkling
2 tbsp water
quick puff pastry (page 30)
milk for glazing

1 Put the apples into a large pan and add the sugar and water. Cover and cook gently, stirring, for about 10 minutes until the apples are soft and fluffy. Taste for sweetness and add more sugar if necessary. Turn into a bowl and leave the apples to cool.

2 Divide the pastry into 2 portions, 1 portion slightly larger than the other. Roll out the larger portion on a lightly floured surface and use to line the pie dish.

3 Spoon the apple filling on to the pastry case, spreading it almost to the edge and then doming it in the middle.

4 Roll out the remaining pastry. Brush the edge of the pastry case with a little water, then lay the pastry lid over the apple filling. Trim the edge, then crimp to seal. Make a small hole in the pastry lid to allow the steam to escape.

5 Use the pastry trimmings to make leaves to decorate the pie, attaching them with milk. Brush the pastry lid with milk and sprinkle with sugar.

6 Put the pie dish on a hot baking tray in a preheated oven at 220°C (425°F, Gas 7) and bake for 25–30 minutes until the pastry is golden.

APPLE PIE VARIATIONS

SPICED APPLE PIE

For a change add ½ tsp of cinnamon, ½ tsp mixed spice, and 75g (3oz) sultanas to the apple mixture before spooning into the dish.

CHRISTMAS APPLE PIE

For a treat at Christmas spoon a 450g (1lb) jar of good mincemeat into the dish and spread evenly. Arrange apple on top and continue with the recipe. You may need a slightly deeper dish if adding the mincemeat.

RHUBARB AND ORANGE PIE

When rhubarb is in season, there is nothing nicer – you can use the young, sweet pink rhubarb or older rhubarb but taste for sweetness and add sugar accordingly. Replace the apples with the same amount of fresh rhubarb. Cut into pieces, tip into a pan, add finely grated zest and juice of 1 large orange. Add 1 tbsp of sugar and stew the rhubarb over a low heat for about 10 minutes until just tender. If needed add more sugar. Continue with the recipe.

PLUM PIE

When plums are in season, plum pie is delicious. Replace the apples with the same amount of fresh plums. Cut into halves, remove the stone and stew the plums over a low heat for about 10 minutes until just soft. Taste for sweetness, if a little sharp, sprinkle in a little caster sugar. Continue with the recipe.

clockwise from top left: *Cinnamon sticks, mincemeat, rhubarb, and fresh plums.*

SERVES 6–8

23CM (9IN) FLAN DISH OR TIN

150g (5oz) caster sugar, plus extra
   for sprinkling
45g (1¹/₂oz) cornflour
750g (1¹/₂lb) rhubarb, cut into
   1cm (¹/₂in) slices
1 cinnamon stick, halved
375g (12oz) strawberries,
   hulled and halved

PASTRY

175g (6oz) plain flour
90g (3oz) chilled butter, cubed
about 2 tbsp cold water

STRAWBERRY AND RHUBARB PIE

1 Make the pastry: put the flour into a large bowl, add the butter, and rub in with the fingertips until the mixture resembles fine breadcrumbs. Add enough water to bind to a soft, but not sticky dough. On a lightly floured surface, divide the dough in half and roll out one half into a thin round to line the bottom and sides of the flan dish. Chill in the refrigerator for about 30 minutes.

2 Meanwhile, combine the sugar with the cornflour and toss with the rhubarb, cinnamon, and strawberries. Leave to soak for 15–20 minutes.

3 Put the soaked fruit into the pastry case, removing the cinnamon.

4 Roll out the second half of pastry to the same size as the first round. Cut a 1cm (¹/₂in) strip from around the edge of the pastry.

5 Cut the remaining pastry into 1cm (¹/₂in) strips and arrange in a lattice on top of the pie. Brush the ends with water and attach the long strip around the rim of the pie. Sprinkle with 1–2 tbsp sugar.

6 Bake on a hot baking tray in a preheated oven at 220°C (425°F, Gas 7) for 10 minutes; reduce the oven temperature to 180°C (350°F, Gas 4), and bake for a further 30–40 minutes until the fruit is just cooked, and the pastry golden. Serve warm or cold.

Hot Puddings

PINEAPPLE UPSIDE-DOWN PUDDING

SERVES 8

18CM (7IN) ROUND CAKE TIN

60g (2oz) butter, softened, plus
  extra for greasing
60g (2oz) light muscovado sugar
1 × 225g (7½oz) can pineapple
  rings in natural juice, drained,
  and juice reserved
4 ready-to-eat dried apricots,
  coarsely chopped

SPONGE

125g (4oz) butter, softened
125g (4oz) caster sugar
2 eggs, beaten
175g (6oz) self-raising flour
1 tsp baking powder

1 Lightly butter the tin and line the bottom with baking parchment. Cream together the butter and sugar and spread evenly over the baking parchment.

2 Arrange the pineapple rings on top of the butter and sugar mixture, and sprinkle the chopped dried apricots between the pineapple rings.

3 Make the sponge: put the butter, caster sugar, eggs, flour, and baking powder into a bowl with 2 tbsp of the reserved pineapple juice. Beat for 2 minutes or until smooth and well blended. Spoon the mixture on top of the pineapple rings and level the surface.

4 Bake in a preheated oven at 180°C (350°F, Gas 4) for about 45 minutes until the sponge is well risen and springy to the touch. Invert the sponge on to a warmed serving plate, and serve at once.

Apricot upside-down pudding

Substitute 1 × 400g (13oz) can apricot halves for the pineapple, and 2 tbsp peeled and chopped stem ginger for the dried apricots.

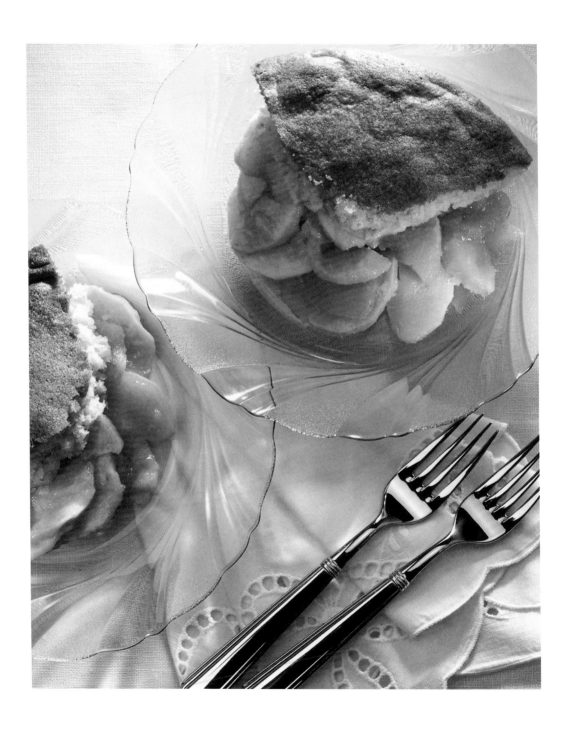

EVE'S PUDDING

SERVES 6

1.25 LITRE (2 PINT) OVENPROOF DISH

butter for greasing
500g (1lb) cooking apples, quartered,
  cored, peeled, and sliced
90g (3oz) demerara sugar
grated zest and juice of 1 lemon

SPONGE TOPPING

125g (4oz) softened butter
125g (4oz) caster sugar
2 eggs, beaten
125g (4oz) self-raising flour
1 tsp baking powder
2 tbsp milk

1 Lightly butter the ovenproof dish and arrange the apples in the bottom. Sprinkle over the demerara sugar and the lemon zest and juice.

2 Make the sponge topping: put the butter, sugar, eggs, flour, baking powder, and milk in a large bowl, and beat until smooth and well blended. Spoon on top of the apple slices, and level the surface.

3 Bake in a preheated oven at 180°C (350°F, Gas 4) for about 45 minutes until the sponge topping is well risen, golden, and springy to the touch. Serve hot.

Cook's know-how

Instead of the demerara sugar on top of the apples, you can use apricot jam, with the grated zest and juice of an orange rather than the lemon. To make a Christmas Eve's Pudding, use mincemeat instead of the sugar or jam, or a mixture of chopped dried cranberries and apricots with 30g (1oz) demerara sugar and a splash of brandy, rum, or sherry.

Spiced eve's pudding

Add 1 tsp ground cinnamon to the sponge topping, and 60g (2oz) raisins, 1 tsp ground cinnamon, and 1tsp ground mixed spice to the apple mixture.

APPLE BROWN BETTY

SERVES 6

DEEP 1.5–2 LITRE (2½–3½ PINT) OVENPROOF DISH

30–45g (1–1½oz) butter
175g (6oz) fresh breadcrumbs
1kg (2lb) cooking apples, quartered,
  cored, peeled, and thinly sliced
125g (4oz) caster sugar, plus
  extra for sprinkling
1 tbsp lemon juice
1–2 tsp ground cinnamon

1 Melt the butter in a frying pan. Add the breadcrumbs and stir over a medium heat for 5 minutes or until the crumbs are crisp and golden. Remove from the heat.

2 Toss the apples with the caster sugar, lemon juice, and ground cinnamon.

3 Press one-quarter of the crisp breadcrumbs over the bottom of the dish. Cover with half of the apple mixture and sprinkle with a further one-quarter of the breadcrumbs.

4 Arrange the remaining apple mixture on top of the breadcrumbs, spoon over any juices, and cover with the remaining breadcrumbs. Sprinkle the top of the pudding lightly with caster sugar.

5 Cover the dish with foil. Bake in a preheated oven at 200°C (400°F, Gas 6) for about 20 minutes.

6 Remove the foil and continue baking for a further 20 minutes or until the apples are tender and the top is golden brown. Serve warm.

Cook's know-how

White or brown bread can be used for the breadcrumbs. Wholemeal gives a nutty flavour, and granary gives an interesting texture. For best results, the bread should be about 2 days old.

SERVES 8

DEEP 18CM (7IN) SQUARE CAKE TIN

90g (3oz) butter, softened, plus
  extra for greasing
150g (5oz) light muscovado sugar
2 eggs, beaten
175g (6oz) self-raising flour
1 tsp baking powder
175g (6oz) stoned dates, roughly chopped
90g (3oz) walnuts, roughly chopped
175ml (6fl oz) hot water

TOFFEE SAUCE

125g (4oz) butter
175g (6oz) light muscovado sugar
6 tbsp double cream
60g (2oz) walnuts, roughly chopped

STICKY TOFFEE PUDDING

1 Butter the cake tin and line the bottom with baking parchment.

2 Put the butter, sugar, eggs, flour, and baking powder into a large bowl. Beat well until smooth and thoroughly blended.

3 Stir in the dates and walnuts, and then the measured hot water. Pour the mixture into the tin.

4 Bake in a preheated oven at 180°C (350°F, Gas 4) for 45–50 minutes until the pudding is well risen, browned on top, and springy to the touch.

5 About 10 minutes before the pudding is ready, make the toffee sauce: put the butter and sugar into a small saucepan, and heat gently, stirring, until the butter has melted and the sugar dissolved. Stir in the cream and walnuts and heat gently to warm through.

6 Cut the pudding into 8 even-sized squares, and transfer to serving plates. Spoon over the toffee sauce, and serve at once.

Cook's know-how

Serve the toffee sauce with other hot or cold desserts, such as steamed puddings or ice cream.

RICE PUDDING

SERVES 4

900ML (1½ PINT) OVENPROOF DISH

15g (½oz) butter, plus extra
  for greasing
60g (2oz) short-grain (pudding) rice
600ml (1 pint) full cream milk
30g (1oz) caster sugar
1 strip of lemon zest
¼ tsp grated nutmeg

1 Lightly butter the ovenproof dish. Rinse the rice under cold running water and drain well.

2 Put the rice into the dish and stir in the milk. Leave for about 30 minutes to allow the rice to soften.

3 Add the caster sugar and lemon zest to the rice mixture, and stir to mix. Sprinkle the surface of the milk with freshly grated nutmeg and dot with small knobs of butter.

4 Bake in a preheated oven at 150°C (300°F, Gas 2) for about 2–2½ hours until the skin of the pudding is brown. Serve at once.

Cook's know-how

Pudding rice has short, rounded grains, which absorb the milk to give a rich, creamy consistency. If you don't have full cream milk, use cream and semi-skimmed milk.

Chilled rice with pears

Let the pudding cool, then lift off the skin. Chill the pudding and serve in glass dishes, topped with slices of poached fresh or canned pears, topped with melted strawberry jam.

KEY TECHNIQUES

STEAMED PUDDINGS

Light sponges and rich suet mixtures can both be gently cooked by steaming. Be sure to make the seal tight so moisture cannot get inside. It is important to keep the water in the saucepan topped up, so boil some water ready to add to the pan when needed. Use this technique when making Steamed Jam Pudding (page 84), Christmas Pudding (page 88), and Treacle and Orange Pudding (page 108).

1 Turn the mixture into a greased, heatproof bowl. Layer a piece of greaseproof paper with a piece of foil and make a pleat across the middle, to allow for the pudding's expansion during cooking. Butter the paper.

2 Place the foil and paper, buttered-side down, over the top of the bowl. Secure by tying string tightly under the rim. Form a handle with another piece of string across the top of the foil. Trim away excess paper and foil.

far right: Ensure the water is simmering so that when you lower the pudding in it starts to cook straight away.

3 Put a trivet or metal jam jar lid in the bottom of a saucepan and half fill with water. Bring to a simmer. Lower the bowl into the saucepan; add more boiling water to come halfway up the side of the bowl. Cover tightly and steam for the required time. Make sure that the water stays at simmering point and top up when necessary.

SERVES 4–6

1.25 LITRE (2 PINT) PUDDING BOWL

125g (4oz) soft butter or margarine,
  plus extra for greasing
3 tbsp jam
125g (4oz) caster sugar
2 eggs, beaten
175g (6oz) self-raising flour
1 tsp baking powder
about 1 tbsp milk

STEAMED JAM PUDDING

1 Lightly butter the pudding bowl, and spoon the jam into the bottom.

2 Put the butter or margarine, sugar, eggs, flour, and baking powder into a large bowl, and beat until smooth and thoroughly blended. Add enough milk to give a dropping consistency.

3 Spoon the mixture into the pudding bowl, and smooth the surface. Cover with buttered greaseproof paper and foil, both pleated in the middle. Secure with string (page 82).

4 Put the bowl into a steamer or saucepan of simmering water, making sure the water comes halfway up the side of the bowl. Cover and steam, topping up with boiling water as needed, for about 1½ hours. Turn the pudding out on to a warmed plate, and serve hot.

STEAMED PUDDING VARIATIONS

TOFFEE APPLE STEAMED PUDDING

You will need a slightly large basin if adding fruit. Peel and remove the core from 450g (1lb) dessert apples, cut into raisin sized cubes. Transfer to a saucepan. Add 25g (1oz) butter and 100g (4oz) Demerara sugar. Heat gently, stirring until the butter and sugar have dissolved. Pour into the base of the prepared basin. Continue with the recipe omitting the jam.

SYRUP STEAMED PUDDING

Pour 4 tbsp of golden syrup into the base of the pudding basin. Continue with the recipe, omitting the jam. To make extra special, turn out the pudding and just before serving pour over some more heated golden syrup.

LEMON STEAMED PUDDING

Replace the jam with 3 tbsp of luxury lemon curd. Add finely grated zest of 2 lemons to the sponge mixture. Continue with the recipe.

DOUBLE APRICOT STEAMED PUDDING

Replace the jam with 3 tbsp of apricot jam. Stir in 50g (2oz) chopped dried apricots and 25g (1oz) sultanas into the sponge mixture. Continue with the recipe.

clockwise from top left: *Dessert apples, golden syrup, lemon and zest, and apricot jam.*

CHRISTMAS PUDDING

SERVES 8–10

1.25 LITRE (2 PINT) PUDDING BOWL

90g (3oz) self-raising flour
125g (4oz) shredded vegetable suet
  or grated chilled butter
30g (1oz) blanched almonds,
  shredded or chopped
125g (4oz) carrot, grated
250g (8oz) raisins
125g (4oz) currants
125g (4oz) sultanas
125g (4oz) fresh breadcrumbs
¼ tsp grated nutmeg
60g (2oz) mixed candied peel, chopped
90g (3oz) light muscovado sugar
grated zest and juice of 1 lemon
2 eggs, beaten
butter for greasing
75ml (2½fl oz) dark rum or brandy

BRANDY BUTTER

250g (8oz) unsalted butter
250g (8oz) caster sugar or icing sugar
90ml (3fl oz) brandy

1 In a large bowl, combine the flour, suet or butter, almonds, carrot, raisins, currants, sultanas, breadcrumbs, nutmeg, candied peel, sugar, and lemon zest. Add the lemon juice and eggs, and stir until well combined.

2 Lightly butter the pudding bowl. Spoon in the pudding mixture and level the surface.

3 Cover with buttered greaseproof paper, then foil, both pleated in the middle. Secure the paper and foil in place by tying string under the rim of the bowl (page 82).

4 Put the bowl into a steamer or saucepan of simmering water, making sure the water comes halfway up the side of the bowl. Cover and steam, adding more boiling water as needed, for 6 hours.

5 Remove the bowl from the steamer or pan and leave to cool. Remove the paper and foil covering. The pudding should be a dark rich brown colour. Make a few holes in the pudding with a fine skewer, and pour in the rum or brandy. Cover the pudding with fresh greaseproof paper and foil. Store in a cool place for up to 3 months.

6 Make the brandy butter: cream together all the ingredients. It can be stored, frozen, for 3 months.

7 To reheat the pudding for serving, steam for 2–3 hours. Serve at once, with the brandy butter.

APPLE CHARLOTTE

SERVES 6

15CM (6IN) SQUARE CAKE TIN

1kg (2lb) cooking apples, quartered,
  cored, peeled, and sliced
125g (4oz) caster sugar
3 tbsp water
2 tbsp apricot jam
125g (4oz) butter, softened,
  plus extra for greasing
12 thin slices of white bread,
  crusts removed

1 Put the apples, sugar, and measured water in a saucepan and cook over a medium heat for about 10–15 minutes until the apples are soft but still holding their shape. Stir in the apricot jam.

2 Spread the butter on one side of each slice of bread. Lightly butter the cake tin. Use 8 of the bread slices to line the tin, cutting them into strips or squares as necessary, and placing them buttered-side down. Spoon in the apple mixture. Cut the remaining slices of bread into quarters diagonally. Arrange the quarters, buttered-side up, on top of the apple mixture.

3 Bake in a preheated oven at 200°C (400°F, Gas 6) for about 40 minutes until crisp and golden. Serve hot.

SAUCES FOR PUDDINGS

As well as adding moisture to baked desserts, a sauce also gives an interesting texture combination on the palette. Try these sauces with Classic Apple Crumble (page 40), Blackberry and Apple Cobbler (page 42), Double Crust Apple Pie (page 64), Strawberry and Rhubarb Pie (page 68), Steamed Jam Pudding (page 84), Rich Bread and Butter Pudding (page 106), and Treacle and Orange Pudding (page 108).

SWEET WHITE

Blend 1 tbsp cornflour with 1 tbsp caster sugar, and a little milk taken from 300ml (½ pint). Bring the remaining milk to a boil and stir into the cornflour mixture. Return to the saucepan and heat gently, stirring, until thickened. If preferred, add flavourings such as grated orange zest, brandy, rum, or vanilla extract to the sauce. Serve warm.

SABAYON

Put 4 egg yolks, 60g (2oz) caster sugar, and 150ml (¼ pint) dry white wine into a bowl over a saucepan of gently simmering water. Whisk for 5–8 minutes or until the mixture is frothy and thick. Remove from the heat and whisk in the grated zest of 1 orange. Serve at once or, to serve cool, continue whisking the mixture until cool.

CUSTARD

Blend together 3 eggs, 30g (1oz) caster sugar, and 1 tsp cornflour. Heat 600ml (1 pint) full cream milk to just below boiling and stir into the eggs. Return to the pan and heat gently, stirring, until thickened. Strain into a cold bowl. Serve warm or cold. Use 300ml (½ pint) each of cream and milk for a richer custard.

Far right: The consistency of custard is a matter of preference. Alter the quantity of milk to find your perfect pour.

BAKLAVA

MAKES 20 SQUARES

SHALLOW 18 × 23CM (7 × 9IN) RECTANGULAR CAKE TIN

250g (8oz) walnut pieces, finely chopped
60g (2oz) light muscovado sugar
1 tsp ground cinnamon
175g (6oz) butter, melted, plus
  extra for greasing
24 sheets of filo pastry, weighing
  about 500g (1lb)
90ml (3fl oz) clear honey
2 tbsp lemon juice

1 Mix together the walnuts, sugar, and cinnamon. Lightly butter the cake tin and lay 1 sheet of filo pastry in the bottom of the tin, allowing the pastry to come up the sides. (If necessary, cut the sheets in half to fit in the tin.) Brush the pastry with a little melted butter.

2 Repeat with 5 more filo sheets, layering and brushing each one with the butter. Sprinkle with one-third of the nut mixture.

3 Repeat this process twice, using 6 more sheets of filo pastry each time, brushing each sheet with butter and sprinkling the nut mixture over each sixth sheet. Finish with 6 buttered sheets of filo pastry, and lightly brush the top with melted butter.

4 Trim the edges of the filo, then, using a sharp knife, cut about halfway through the pastry layers to make 20 squares.

5 Bake in a preheated oven at 220°C (425°F, Gas 7) for 15 minutes, then reduce the oven temperature to 180°C (350°F, Gas 4) and bake for 10–15 minutes until the pastry is crisp and golden brown. Remove the baklava from the oven.

6 Heat the honey and lemon juice in a heavy saucepan until the honey has melted. Spoon over the hot baklava. Leave to cool in the tin for 1–2 hours. Cut into the marked squares, and serve the baklava at room temperature or reheat until just hot.

MAGIC CHOCOLATE PUDDING

SERVES 4

1 LITRE (1¾ PINT) OVENPROOF DISH

60g (2oz) caster sugar
60g (2oz) fine semolina
30g (1oz) cocoa powder
1 tsp baking powder
30g (1oz) butter, melted,
  plus extra for greasing
2 eggs, beaten
½ tsp vanilla extract
icing sugar for dusting

SAUCE

90g (3oz) light muscovado sugar
2 tbsp cocoa powder
300ml (½ pint) hot water

1 Mix together the sugar and semolina in a large bowl. Sift the cocoa powder and baking powder into the bowl, and mix thoroughly.

2 In a separate bowl, whisk together the melted butter, eggs, and vanilla extract with an electric whisk. Add this mixture to the dry ingredients and stir with a wooden spoon until well blended.

3 Lightly butter the ovenproof dish. Pour the mixture into the dish.

4 Make the sauce: mix together the muscovado sugar and cocoa powder, and gradually stir in the measured hot water. Pour the liquid over the pudding.

5 Bake the pudding in a preheated oven at 180°C (350°F, Gas 4) for 30 minutes or until the liquid has sunk to the bottom and the sponge is well risen and springy to the touch. Sprinkle with icing sugar, and serve at once.

Nutty chocolate pudding

For a crunchier pudding, add 60g (2oz) chopped pecan nuts or walnuts to the dry ingredients in step 1.

SERVES 4

2 × 4-HOLE NON-STICK YORKSHIRE PUDDING TINS

60g (2oz) butter, softened, plus
  extra for greasing
60g (2oz) caster sugar
2 eggs, beaten
60g (2oz) self-raising flour
300ml (½ pint) milk
apricot jam and caster sugar to serve

FRENCH PANCAKES

1 Combine the butter and sugar in a bowl and cream together until soft. Beat in the eggs, a little at a time, then fold in the flour.

2 In a small saucepan, heat the milk to just below boiling point. Stir into the creamed mixture.

3 Lightly butter the yorkshire pudding tins, and divide the batter equally among them. Bake in a preheated oven at 190°C (375°F, Gas 5) for about 20 minutes until the pancakes are well risen and golden brown.

4 Slide the pancakes out of the tins, and serve with apricot jam and caster sugar. Serve with the apricot jam and sprinkle with sugar.

CRÊPES SUZETTE

SERVES 4

18–20CM (7–8IN) FRYING PAN

125g (4oz) plain flour
1 egg
1 tbsp oil, plus extra for frying
300ml (½ pint) milk

ORANGE SAUCE

juice of 2 oranges
125g (4oz) unsalted butter
60g (2oz) caster sugar
3–4 tbsp orange liqueur or brandy

1 Make the crêpes: sift the flour into a bowl. Make a well in the middle. Mix together the egg, 1 tbsp oil, and the milk, and pour into the well. Gradually beat in the flour, to make a fairly thin batter.

2 Heat a little oil in the frying pan, then wipe away the excess oil. Add 2–3 tbsp batter to the pan, tilting it to coat the bottom evenly. Cook for 45–60 seconds, then turn over, and cook the other side for about 30 seconds. Slide the crêpe out on to a warmed plate.

3 Repeat to make 7 more crêpes. Stack the crêpes on top of each other as soon as they are cooked (they will not stick together).

4 Put the orange juice, butter, sugar, and liqueur or brandy into a large frying pan, and boil for 5 minutes until reduced. Place 1 crêpe in the pan, coat with sauce, fold in half, then in half again. Move to one side of the pan. Add another crêpe. Coat with the sauce, and fold as before. Repeat with the remaining crêpes. Heat to warm through.

FRUIT FRITTERS

SERVES 6

2 apples
3 bananas
juice of ½ lemon
sunflower oil for deep-frying
60g (2oz) caster sugar
1 tsp ground cinnamon

BATTER

125g (4oz) plain flour
1 tbsp icing sugar
1 egg, separated
150ml (¼ pint) mixed milk and water

1 Quarter, core, and peel the apples. Cut the apples and bananas into bite-sized pieces. Toss the pieces in the lemon juice to prevent discoloration.

2 Make the batter: sift the flour and sugar into a bowl, and make a well. Add the egg yolk and a little of the milk mixture and whisk together. Whisk in half of the remaining milk mixture, drawing in the flour to form a smooth batter. Add the remaining milk.

3 Whisk the egg white in a separate clean bowl until stiff but not dry. Fold into the batter until evenly mixed.

4 Heat the oil in a deep-fat fryer to 190°C (375°F). Pat the fruit dry. Dip each piece of fruit into the batter, lower into the hot oil, and cook in batches for 3–4 minutes until golden and crisp. Drain on paper towels and keep warm while cooking the remainder.

5 Combine the caster sugar and cinnamon, sprinkle generously over the fritters, and serve at once.

Cook's know-how

For a light, crisp batter, the egg white should be whisked and folded in just before you are ready to cook the fritters – don't leave the batter to stand or it will lose its airy texture.

JAMAICAN BANANAS

SERVES 4

30–45g (1–1½oz) unsalted butter
2–3 tbsp light muscovado sugar
½ tsp ground cinnamon
60ml (2fl oz) dark rum
4 firm but ripe bananas, cut in
  half lengthways
vanilla ice cream to serve

1 Put the butter and sugar into a large heavy frying pan, and heat gently until the butter has melted and sugar dissolved. Stir to blend together, then cook gently, stirring, for about 5 minutes.

2 Stir the cinnamon and rum into the caramel mixture, then add the banana halves. Cook for 3 minutes on each side until warmed through.

3 Transfer the bananas and hot sauce to serving plates. Serve at once, with scoops of vanilla ice cream.

Cook's know-how

If you want to serve these bananas to children, use the freshly squeezed juice of an orange instead of the rum, plus the grated orange zest if you think they will like it. In summer you could bake the bananas wrapped in foil on the barbecue and make the sauce separately.

RICH BREAD AND BUTTER PUDDING

SERVES 6

1.7 LITRE (3 PINT) OVENPROOF DISH

12 thin slices of white bread,
  crusts removed
about 125g (4oz) butter, softened,
  plus extra for greasing
85g (3oz) currants
85g (3oz) sultanas
grated zest of 2 lemons
125g (4oz) demerara sugar
300ml (½ pint) milk
300ml (½ pint) double cream
2 eggs

1 Spread one side of each slice of bread with a thick layer of butter. Cut each slice of bread in half diagonally. Lightly butter the ovenproof dish and arrange 12 of the triangles, buttered-side down, in the bottom of the dish.

2 Sprinkle over half of the dried fruit, lemon zest, and sugar. Top with the remaining bread, buttered-side up. Sprinkle over the remaining fruit, lemon zest, and sugar.

3 Beat together the milk, cream, and eggs, and strain over the bread. Leave for 1 hour so that the bread can absorb some of the liquid.

4 Bake in a preheated oven at 180°C (350°F, Gas 4) for about 40 minutes until the bread slices on the top of the pudding are a golden brown colour and crisp, and the custard mixture has set completely. Serve at once.

Bread and butter pudding with marmalade

Spread 6 of the slices of bread with thick-cut marmalade after spreading all of them with the butter. Halve the slices, and arrange the buttered ones buttered-side down in the dish. Sprinkle with the dried fruit, lemon zest, and sugar, then arrange the remaining triangles, marmalade-side up, on top.

SERVES 4–6

900ML (1½ PINT) PUDDING BOWL

butter for greasing
90ml (3fl oz) golden syrup
125g (4oz) self-raising flour
125g (4oz) shredded vegetable suet
  or grated chilled butter
125g (4oz) fresh white breadcrumbs
60g (2oz) caster sugar
grated rind of 2 oranges
about 125ml (4fl oz) milk

SAUCE

juice of 2 oranges
90ml (3fl oz) golden syrup

TREACLE AND ORANGE PUDDING

1 Lightly butter the bowl and spoon the golden syrup into the bottom.

2 Put the flour, suet or butter, breadcrumbs, sugar, and orange rind into a bowl and stir to combine. Stir in enough milk to give a dropping consistency. Spoon into the bowl on top of the syrup.

3 Cover the bowl with buttered baking parchment and foil, both pleated in the middle. Secure by tying string under the rim of the bowl (page 82).

4 Put the bowl into a steamer or saucepan of simmering water, making sure the water comes halfway up the side of the bowl if using a saucepan. Cover and steam, topping up with boiling water as needed, for about 3 hours. Turn out the pudding, and serve with the heated golden syrup and orange juice as a sauce and custard (page 92) if desired.

Chilled and Fruity Desserts

GOOSEBERRY FOOL

SERVES 6

500g (1lb) gooseberries, topped
   and tailed
1 tbsp water
60g (2oz) butter
2 elderflower heads (optional)
caster sugar to taste
300ml (½ pint) double cream,
   whipped until thick
strips of blanched lime zest to decorate

1 Put the gooseberries into a pan with the measured water, butter, and elderflowers, if using. Cover and cook gently for 5–10 minutes until the gooseberries are soft.

2 Remove the eldeflower heads with a slotted spoon. Purée in a food processor until smooth. Add sugar to taste and leave to cool.

3 Fold mixture into cream. Turn into serving glasses and chill for 30 minutes. Decorate with lime zest.

RASPBERRY FOOL

Omit the gooseberry and elderflower. Purée 500g (1lb) fresh or frozen raspberries in a processor or blender until smooth. Sieve into a bowl and add 1 tbsp icing sugar to taste. Continue with the recipe.

APRICOT FOOL

When in season fresh apricots are wonderful. Omit the gooseberry and elderflower. Quarter 500g (1lb) fresh apricots and remove the stones. Tip into a pan, add the peel of one lemon and 1 tbsp of caster sugar. Heat gently over a low heat for about 10 minutes until just soft. Discard the lemon peel and purée in a processor or blender until smooth. Sieve into a bowl and taste, if a little sharp add a little more sugar. Continue with the recipe.

BLACKBERRY FOOL

Omit the gooseberry and elderflower. Measure 750g (1½lb) fresh blackberries into a pan, add 175g (6oz) caster sugar and 2 tbsp of lemon juice. Heat over a medium heat for about 10 minutes until just soft. Purée in a processor or blender until smooth. Sieve into a bowl, taste for sweetness. Continue with the recipe.

clockwise from top left: *Freshly picked raspberries, apricots, and blackberries.*

TROPICAL FRUIT CHEESECAKE

SERVES 10

23CM (9IN) LOOSE-BOTTOMED OR SPRINGFORM CAKE TIN

2 ripe mangoes
150ml (¼ pint) mango or orange
  juice from a carton
15g (½oz) powdered gelatine
250g (8oz) full-fat soft cheese,
  at room temperature
125g (4oz) caster sugar
2 eggs, separated
150ml (¼ pint) whipping cream,
  whipped until thick

BISCUIT BASE

125g (4oz) digestive biscuits, crushed
60g (2oz) butter, melted
30g (1oz) demerara sugar

DECORATION

2 kiwi fruit, peeled and sliced
1 × 250g (8oz) can pineapple pieces
  in natural juice, drained

1 Make the biscuit base: mix together the biscuits, butter, and sugar, and press over the tin's base.

2 Slice the mango flesh away from the stones (page 146). Peel, then purée in a food processor.

3 Pour 5 tbsp of the fruit juice into a heatproof bowl, and sprinkle in the gelatine. Leave for about 10 minutes until it becomes spongy. Stand the bowl in a small pan of hot water, and heat gently until the gelatine has dissolved. Add the remaining fruit juice.

4 In a large bowl, beat the soft cheese until smooth and creamy. Beat in half of the caster sugar, the egg yolks, and the mango purée. Gradually beat in the gelatine mixture.

5 In a separate bowl, whisk the egg whites until stiff but not dry. Whisk in the remaining sugar, 1 tsp at a time, and continue to whisk at high speed until the sugar is incorporated and the mixture stiff and glossy.

6 Fold the whipped cream into the cheese and mango mixture, then fold in the egg whites. Pour on to the biscuit base and chill until set.

7 Use a knife to loosen the side of the cheesecake, then remove from the tin. Slide on to a serving plate. Decorate the top with slices of kiwi fruit and pieces of pineapple before serving.

KEY TECHNIQUES

DISSOLVING GELATINE

Gelatine is a flavourless setting agent used in chilled desserts such as fruit jellies. It is most commonly available as a powder, in sachets. Leaf gelatine can also be used (4 sheets in place of 1 sachet): soften in cold water for 5 minutes, then drain and melt in the hot dessert mixture, whisking well. Use this technique when making Tropical Fruit Cheesecake (page 116), Chilled Lemon Soufflé (page 120), Cranberry and Vodka Jelly (page 126), Port and Claret Jelly (page 128), and Marbled Raspberry Cheesecake (page 138).

1 Put the given quantity of cold water or other liquid into a small heatproof bowl and sprinkle the given quantity of gelatine over the surface. Leave to soak for about 10 minutes until the gelatine has absorbed the liquid and becomes spongy.

2 Put the bowl of gelatine into a pan of hot water and heat until the gelatine has dissolved and is clear. Use a metal spoon to check that there are no granules left. Use the gelatine at the same temperature as the mixture it is setting.

WHISKING EGG WHITES

A balloon whisk is the classic tool for whisking egg whites, but an electric mixer saves time and effort. Ensure all your equipment is clean, dry, and grease-free, and that the egg whites are at room temperature.

Whisk quickly
Whisk the whites as forcefully as possible (on maximum speed if using an electric mixer) right from the start. When they look like a cloud, add any sugar little by little. The mixture will get stiffer and stiffer as you add sugar and whisk.

FOLDING EGG WHITES

To retain as much air as possible, egg whites should be folded gently and quickly into a mixture using a metal spoon or a rubber spatula, not a wooden spoon.

Fold gradually
Mix a spoonful of the whites into the heavy mixture to lighten it. Using a rubber spatula or metal spoon, fold in the remaining whites using a "figure of eight" motion, cutting straight through the mixture, then turning it over until well blended.

CHILLED LEMON SOUFFLÉ

SERVES 4

1 LITRE (1¾ PINT) SOUFFLÉ DISH

3 tbsp cold water
15g (½oz) powdered gelatine
3 large eggs, separated
250g (8oz) caster sugar
grated zest and juice of 3 lemons
300ml (½ pint) double or whipping cream,
  whipped until thick

DECORATION

30g (1oz) nibbed almonds, lightly toasted
150ml (¼ pint) double or whipping cream,
  whipped until stiff

1 Prepare the soufflé dish: tie a band of double thickness greaseproof paper or foil around the outside so that it stands about 5cm (2in) above the top of the dish. Fold in half. Wrap around the dish and secure with tape or string.

2 Put the water into a small bowl and sprinkle the gelatine over the top. Leave for about 10 minutes until it becomes spongy. Stand in a pan of hot water and heat until dissolved.

3 Put the egg yolks and sugar into a heatproof bowl and put over a pan of gently simmering water. Do not let the bottom of the bowl touch the water. Using an electric hand-held mixer, whisk together. Add the lemon zest and juice and whisk at full speed until the mixture is pale and thick.

4 Fold the whipped cream into the lemon mixture, then fold in the dissolved gelatine.

5 In a separate large bowl, whisk the egg whites until stiff but not dry. Fold into the lemon mixture, and carefully pour into the prepared soufflé dish. Level the surface, then chill for about 4 hours until set.

6 Carefully remove the paper collar. Decorate the outside edge of the soufflé with the lightly toasted almonds and sprinkle some in the middle. Pipe the cream (page 185) around the edge of the soufflé, and serve chilled.

PASSION FRUIT SOUFFLÉ

Omit the lemon zest and juice. Replace with juice and pips of 6 fresh passion fruit. Continue with the recipe.

STRAWBERRY SOUFFLÉ

Omit the lemon zest and juice. Purée 500g (1lb) fresh strawberries in a processor or blender. At step 4 fold in the strawberry purée after adding the cream.

LEMON AND LIME SOUFFLÉ

Replace the lemons in the recipe with the finely grated zest and juice of 2 limes and 1 large lemon. Continue with the recipe.

clockwise from top left: *Passion fruit, strawberries, and limes.*

JUBILEE TRIFLE

SERVES 6

6 INDIVIDUAL GLASS DISHES, OR A 1.5 LITRE (2⅓ PINT)
   SHALLOW GLASS DISH, ABOUT 20CM (8IN) IN DIAMETER

8 trifle sponges
about 7 tbsp black cherry jam
1 × 420g (13½oz) can pear quarters
   in natural juice, drained and juice
   reserved
1 × 420g (13½oz) can stoned cherries,
   drained and juice reserved
4 tbsp kirsch or other cherry liqueur
500ml (18fl oz) custard (ready made
   or see page 92 and use double the
   amount of cornflour)
150ml (¼ pint) whipping cream

1 Split the trifle sponges in half, spread generously with about 4 tbsp jam, and sandwich together again. Place 4 in the bottom of 6 individual glass dishes, cutting them to fit.

2 Chop each pear quarter into small pieces, and arrange some of the pieces around the edges of the glass dishes, and some in between the sponges. Dot with the cherries.

3 Mix the 5 tbsp of the pear juice with the kirsch, and pour half of it over the sponges. Arrange the last four sponges in the dishes, again cutting them to fit, then pour over the remaining juice and kirsch. Leave for a few minutes, then gently squash flat with the back of a spoon. Pour over the custard, level gently, and chill for 1 hour.

4 Lightly whip the cream – it should still be soft and floppy – and spread over the custard. Cover and chill for at least 4 hours (or up to 24 hours).

5 To serve, warm 3 tbsp cherry jam in a small pan with 2 tbsp of the reserved cherry juice until the jam has dissolved. Leave to cool, then sieve to remove any lumps, and drizzle over the trifles.

clockwise from top left: *Port and Claret Jelly, Raspberry Passion, Cranberry and Vodka Jelly, Jubilee Trifle.*

CRANBERRY AND VODKA JELLY

SERVES 4

4 × 100ML (3½FL OZ) GLASSES

2 sheets of leaf gelatine
175ml (6fl oz) cranberry juice
125ml (4fl oz) vodka
squeeze of lime juice
small red fruits (eg raspberries, cherries, redcurrants, wild strawberries) to serve

1 Put the sheets of gelatine into a medium bowl and cover with cold water. Leave to soak for about 5 minutes until softened.

2 Heat the cranberry juice in a pan. Lift the gelatine out of the water, squeeze it, then add to the cranberry juice and stir until the gelatine has dissolved. Cool slightly, then add the vodka and lime juice. Cool completely, then pour into glasses, cover and chill until set, about 6 hours. Serve topped with small red fruits.

Illustrated on page 125.

Cook's know-how

If you want to use powdered gelatine instead of gelatine leaves, you will need to sprinkle 1½ tsp gelatine powder over 1½ tbsp cold water. Leave to sponge for 10 minutes before stirring into the hot liquid.

The sharp taste of cranberry is a wonderful addition to a vodka dessert.

SERVES 8

1.5 LITRE (2½ PINT) JELLY MOULD OR 8 WINE GLASSES

8 sheets of leaf gelatine
   (about 25g/scant 1oz)
250g (8oz) caster sugar
450ml (¾ pint) water
2 tbsp redcurrant jelly
1 cinnamon stick
450ml (¾ pint) claret
300ml (½ pint) ruby port

TO SERVE

small seasonal red fruits, eg raspberries,
   cherries, redcurrants, wild strawberries
cream (optional)

PORT AND CLARET JELLY

1 Put the sheets of gelatine in a bowl and cover with cold water. Soak for 5 minutes until soft.

2 Meanwhile, put the sugar into a large saucepan, pour in the water, and add the jelly. Heat gently until the sugar and jelly have dissolved, then add the cinnamon stick, claret, and port. Bring to a boil, bubble for 1 minute, then take the pan off the heat.

3 Pour the wine through a sieve lined with a double layer of muslin (or a J-cloth) into a bowl. Lift the gelatine out of the water, squeeze it, then add to the wine and stir until the gelatine has dissolved. Cool a little, pour into a mould or glasses, and leave until cold. Cover, and chill until set, at least 4 hours. Serve with seasonal fruits, and cream if you like.

Illustrated on page 125.

Cook's know-how
To use powdered gelatine instead of gelatine leaves, you will need to sprinkle 2 tbsp gelatine powder over 6 tbsp cold water in a small bowl. Leave to sponge for 10 minutes before stirring into the hot liquid.

Port and claret subdue the tart taste of redurrants, to produce a delicious jelly.

RASPBERRY PASSION

SERVES 6

6 × 300ML (½ PINT) STEMMED GLASSES

3 ripe passion fruit
500g (1lb) plain yogurt
200ml (7fl oz) half-fat crème fraîche
375g (12oz) raspberries
90g (3oz) light muscovado sugar

1 Using a teaspoon, scoop the seeds and flesh from the passion fruit into a bowl, and mix with the yogurt and crème fraîche.

2 Put an equal quantity of raspberries in each glass, then fill with the crème fraîche mixture. Cover and refrigerate for up to 8 hours.

3 An hour or so before serving, sprinkle with sugar and return to the refrigerator until ready to serve.

Illustrated on page 125.

Ripen passion fruit on a windowsill until you're ready to use them.

CHERRY CHEESECAKE

SERVES 8

23CM (9IN) SPRINGFORM CAKE TIN

375g (12oz) full-fat soft cheese
125g (4oz) caster sugar
2 eggs, beaten
1 tsp vanilla extract
1 tbsp lemon juice

BISCUIT CASE

175g (6oz) digestive biscuits, crushed
90g (3oz) butter, melted
2 tbsp demerara sugar

TOPPING

1 tsp arrowroot
1 × 400g (13oz) can pitted black cherries
1 tbsp kirsch

1 Make the biscuit case: mix together the crushed biscuits, melted butter, and sugar, and press evenly over the bottom and up the side of the cake tin.

2 Put the soft cheese into a bowl and beat until smooth. Add the caster sugar and beat until well blended. Add the eggs, vanilla extract, and lemon juice. Mix until smooth and creamy.

3 Pour the filling into the biscuit case. Bake in a preheated oven at 180°C (350°F, Gas 4) for 25–30 minutes until just set. Leave to cool completely, then transfer to the refrigerator and leave to chill.

4 Make the topping: dissolve the arrowroot in a little of the cherry juice. Put the cherries and their juice into a small pan and add the arrowroot mixture with the kirsch. Bring to a boil, stirring, until thick. Leave to cool completely.

5 Spoon the cherries on top of the cheese filling. Chill. Use a knife to loosen the side of the cheesecake from the tin, then remove the cheesecake. Serve chilled.

Cook's know-how

Cheesecakes freeze well, but should always be frozen without the topping. Thaw in the refrigerator, then decorate. Fruit toppings may be prepared at the same time and frozen separately. Thaw and add to the cheesecake just before serving.

LEMON SORBET

SERVES 4

SHALLOW FREEZER-PROOF CONTAINER

4 lemons
225g (8oz) caster sugar
600ml (1 pint) water
2 egg whites
lemon zest to decorate

1 Finely grate the zest from the lemons and squeeze out the juice, keep the two separate.

2 Put the sugar and measured water into a saucepan and heat gently until the sugar dissolves. Bring to the boil and leave to boil for 2 minutes. Remove from the heat, add the lemon zest, and leave to cool completely. Stir in the lemon juice.

3 Strain the lemon syrup into the container and freeze for about 2 hours until just mushy. Turn the mixture into a bowl and whisk gently to break down any large crystals.

4 Whisk the egg whites until stiff but not dry, then fold into the mixture. Return to the freezer, and freeze until firm. Transfer the sorbet to the refrigerator to soften for about 30 minutes before serving in scoops and decorate with strips of the lemon zest.

Cook's know-how

Once the sorbet is made, scoop out portions with an ice-cream scoop, pile in a dish and keep in the freezer until ready to serve.

SORBET VARIATIONS

BLACKBERRY SORBET

Replace the lemons with 500g (1lb) blackberries and purée in a food processor. Put 175g (6oz) granulated sugar and 600ml (1 pint) water into a saucepan and heat until the sugar dissolves. Boil for 5 minutes. Stir in blackberry purée and the juice of 1 orange. Pour into a freezerproof container. Continue with the recipe from step 3.

MELON AND MINT SORBET

Replace the lemons with 1 small galia or cantaloupe melon and 2 tbsp chopped fresh mint and purée in a food processor. Put 175g (6oz) granulated sugar and 600ml (1 pint) water into a saucepan and heat until the sugar dissolves. Boil for 5 minutes. Stir in the melon purée and the juice of 1 lemon. Pour into a freezerproof container. Continue with the recipe from step 3.

STRAWBERRY SORBET

Replace the lemons with 500g (1lb) strawberries and purée in a food processor. Put 175g (6oz) granulated sugar and 600ml (1 pint) water into a saucepan and heat until the sugar dissolves. Boil for 5 minutes. Stir in strawberry purée and the juice of 1 orange. Pour into a freezerproof container. Continue with the recipe from step 3.

clockwise from top left: *Fresh blackberries, galia melons, and strawberries.*

SERVES 10

23CM (9IN) LOOSE-BOTTOMED OR
  SPRINGFORM CAKE TIN

3 tbsp cold water
15g (½oz) powdered gelatine
500g (1lb) raspberries
4 tbsp framboise (raspberry liqueur)
250g (8oz) full-fat soft cheese,
  at room temperature
150ml (¼ pint) soured cream
2 eggs, separated
125g (4oz) caster sugar

BISCUIT BASE

125g (4oz) sweet oat or digestive
  biscuits, coarsely crushed
60g (2oz) butter, melted
30g (1oz) demerara sugar
45g (1½oz) walnuts, chopped

DECORATION

150ml (¼ pint) whipping cream,
  whipped until stiff
a few raspberries
mint sprigs

MARBLED RASPBERRY CHEESECAKE

1 Make the biscuit base: mix together the biscuits, butter, demerara sugar, and walnuts and press evenly over the bottom of the tin.

2 Put the measured water into a heatproof bowl, sprinkle the gelatine over the top, and leave for about 10 minutes until spongy.

3 Meanwhile, purée the raspberries in a food processor, then push them through a sieve to remove the seeds. Stir in the liqueur. Set aside.

4 Put the soft cheese into a large bowl, and beat until soft and smooth. Add the soured cream and egg yolks, and beat until well blended.

5 Stand the bowl of gelatine in a saucepan of hot water and heat gently until it dissolves. Stir into the cheese mixture.

6 Make the marbled filling (see overleaf).

7 Use a knife to loosen the side of the cheesecake from the tin, then remove the cheesecake. Slide on to a serving plate. Pipe whipped cream (page 185) around the edge and decorate with raspberries and mint sprigs.

KEY TECHNIQUES

MAKING MARBLED FILLING

Using a marbled filling is an easy way to add style to a cheesecake. Don't overstir the purée and the cheese mixture or you'll lose the marbled effect, as the colours will blend. The quantities in this recipe refers to the Marbled Raspberry Cheesecake (page 138), but you can use the same technique when making Marbled Coffee Ring Cake (page 242).

1 Whisk the egg whites until stiff but not dry. Add the caster sugar, 1 tsp at a time, and whisk until all the sugar is incorporated and the meringue mixture is stiff and glossy.

2 Turn the cheese mixture into the meringue and, using a metal spoon, fold together, blending well. Leave the mixture to chill for about half an hour to thicken slightly.

Far right: Check egg whites are whipped to the correct consistency by lifting the whisk to see if they peak.

3 Fold in the purée, swirling it in just enough to give an attractive marbled effect.

4 Pour the mixture carefully on to the biscuit base and chill in the refrigerator until set.

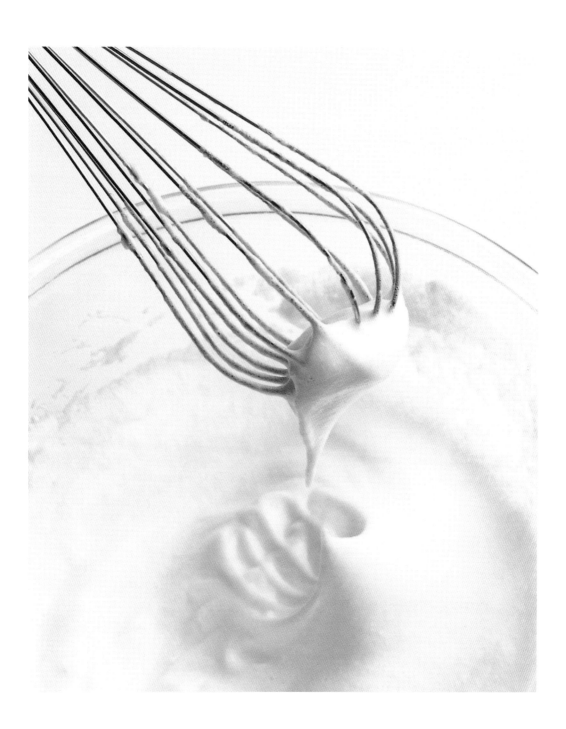

MID-SUMMER PUDDING

SERVES 6

1.25 LITRE (2 PINT) PUDDING BOWL

8 slices of stale medium-sliced white
    bread, crusts removed
200g (8oz) strawberries
200g (8oz) raspberries
200g (8oz) blackcurrants
200g (8oz) redcurrants
150g (5oz) caster sugar
75ml (2½ fl oz) water
2 tbsp framboise or crème de
    cassis liqueur
crème fraîche or Greek yogurt to serve

1 Set 2 slices of bread aside for the top of the pudding, then use the remaining slices to line the bowl: put a slice of bread in the bottom of the bowl, cutting it to fit if necessary, then use the remainder to line the sides. The slices should fit snugly together.

2 Hull and halve the strawberries if large and strip the currants from their stalks.

3 Place the redcurrants and blackcurrants in a saucepan with the sugar and measured water. Heat gently until the juices begin to run. Stir until the sugar has dissolved, and cook until all of the fruit is just tender.

4 Remove from the heat and add the strawberries, raspberries, and liqueur. Spoon the fruit and half of the juice into the lined bowl, reserving the remaining juice. Cover the top of the fruit with the reserved bread slices.

5 Stand the bowl in a shallow dish to catch any juices that may overflow, then put a saucer on top of the bread lid. Place a kitchen weight on top of the saucer. Leave to chill for 8 hours.

6 Invert the pudding on to a serving plate. Spoon the reserved juices over the top, paying attention to pale areas. Serve with either crème fraîche or Greek yogurt.

KEY TECHNIQUES

PREPARING CITRUS FRUITS

There are many ways by which you can infuse the zing of citrus fruits, such as oranges, lemons, and limes, into your desserts. When taking the zest from citrus fruits (even if they are unwaxed), first scrub the fruit with hot soapy water, rinse well, and dry. Use these techniques when preparing Lemon Meringue Pie (page 52), Tarte au Citron (page 58), Treacle and Orange Pudding (page 108), and Chilled Lemon Soufflé (page 120).

Grating
Hold the grater on a plate. Rub the fruit over the medium grid of the grater, removing just the zest and leaving behind the bitter white pith. Use a pastry brush to remove all the zest from the grater.

Zesting
Citrus fruit zest is an attractive garnish. For speedy removal of zest in tiny strips, use a citrus zester or a flat ultra-sharp grater. Hold the fruit in your hand and pull the zester or grater towards you.

Paring
Use a vegetable peeler or small sharp knife to pare off thin strips of zest, trying not to take any of the bitter white pith with it. Cut the pieces of zest lengthways into very fine strips or "julienne".

Peeling

Use a small sharp knife. Cut off a slice of peel across the top and base, cutting through to the flesh. Set the fruit upright on a chopping board and cut away the peel from top to bottom, following the curve of the fruit and cutting away the white pith as well.

Segmenting

Hold the peeled fruit over a bowl to catch the juice. With a sharp knife, cut down one side of a segment, cutting it from the dividing membrane. Cut away from the membrane on the other side, and remove the segment. Continue all around the fruit.

Citrus tips

To get the maximum juice from citrus fruits, first roll the fruit gently on a work surface, pressing lightly. Or heat in the microwave, on HIGH (100% power) for 30 seconds, just until the fruit feels warm. If a recipe includes citrus zest, add it immediately after grating or zesting, preferably to any sugar in the recipe. Then the zest won't discolour or dry out, and all the flavoursome oils from the zest will be absorbed by the sugar.

KEY TECHNIQUES

PREPARING MANGOES

Mangoes have a large, flat central stone and the flesh clings to it tightly. There are 2 methods of preparation, depending on how the flesh is to be used. Use the slicing technique when preparing Tropical Fruit Salad (page 148), in order to get the maximum flesh from your mangoes.

Slicing

For flesh to be used sliced or puréed, cut the flesh from each side of the stone with a sharp knife. Also cut the flesh from the edges of the stone. Then peel and slice or purée.

Dicing

1 Cut the unpeeled flesh away from each side of the stone. Using a sharp knife, carefully score into the flesh in a criss-cross pattern, cutting just to the skin but taking care not to cut through it.

2 Holding the mango in both hands, press in the middle of the skin to open out the cubes of flesh, then cut away from the skin with a sharp knife. For a quick, mobile snack, pull the mango cubes away from the skin with your fingers.

PREPARING A PINEAPPLE

When peeling pineapple, cut away the skin in strips, taking out all the "eyes". If there are any left after peeling, cut them out with the tip of a knife. Use this technique to help you prepare the pineapple in Tropical Fruit Salad (page 148) and Stem Ginger and Pineapple Pavlova (page 206).

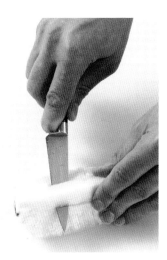

Wedges or cubes
1 Cut off the crown and the base. Stand the pineapple on a chopping board and slice away the skin, from top to bottom.

2 To remove the core, cut the pineapple into quarters lengthways. Cut the central core from each quarter. Cut the quarters as required.

Rings
Do not cut the pineapple lengthways, but, using a sharp knife, cut crossways into 1cm (½in) width slices. Stamp out the central core from each slice using a biscuit or pastry cutter.

TROPICAL FRUIT SALAD

SERVES 6

1 ripe melon eg, Cantaloupe or Ogen
2 ripe mangoes
2 oranges
2 passion fruit
1 ripe papaya (paw paw)
small ripe pineapple

1 Using a sharp knife, cut the melon in half and remove the pips and discard. Remove the skin by cutting between the flesh and the skin and chop into large pieces.

2 Peel the mango and cut in a thick slice either side of the centre stone, cut into large pieces.

3 Using a serrated edged knife, peel and segment the oranges, saving any juice.

4 Cut the passion fruit in half and scoop out the pips and juice.

5 Peel the papaya, take out and discard the seeds using a teaspoon and cut the flesh into pieces.

6 Prepare the pineapple (page 147) and cut into thin wedges or slices.

7 Put all the prepared fruit and any juice into a bowl, cover with clingfilm and refrigerate, mixing from time to time until ready to serve. Serve with crème fraîche or cream if you like.

FRESH FRUIT SALAD VARIATIONS

RED FRUIT SALAD

Put 250g (8oz) each fresh redcurrants and blackberries, and 100g (4oz) blackcurrants into a stainless steel pan with 5 tbsp water. Cook gently for about 5–10 minutes or until just soft. Remove from the heat, stir in 60g (2oz) caster sugar, and leave until the sugar has dissolved and the mixture has cooled slightly (do not add the sugar at the beginning or it will make the skins tough). Add 250g (8oz) strawberries (hulled and halved if large) and 300g (10oz) raspberries to the pan, stir, and tip into a serving dish. Cover and chill in the refrigerator for at least an hour (or overnight) to allow the juices to develop.

DRIED FRUIT SALAD

Put 100g (4oz) each ready to eat dried apricots, prunes, peaches, and figs into a saucepan with about 900ml (1½ pints) cranberry juice. Bring to a boil and simmer gently for about 15 minutes. Add 75g (2½oz) each dried cranberries and blueberries to the pan, and continue cooking for about 15 minutes, adding a little water if necessary. Serve cold or hot in the winter.

top: *Redcurrants and blackcurrants.*
bottom: *Dried apricots, prunes, dates, and figs.*

Chilled and Creamy Desserts

OLD ENGLISH TRIFLE

SERVES 8

1 × 400g (13oz) can white peach
  or pear halves
6 trifle sponges
4 tbsp strawberry or raspberry jam
60g (2oz) ratafia biscuits or macaroons
75ml (2½fl oz) sherry

CUSTARD

3 egg yolks
30g (1oz) caster sugar
1 tsp cornflour
300ml (½ pint) milk

TOPPING

300ml (½ pint) double or whipping cream
30g (1oz) flaked almonds, toasted,
  to decorate

1 Drain and slice the fruit, reserving the juice.

2 Cut the trifle sponges in half horizontally and sandwich the halves together with the jam.

3 Line the bottom of a glass serving bowl with the trifle sponges, and arrange the fruit and biscuits on top. Drizzle over the sherry and reserved fruit juice, and leave to soak while you make the custard.

4 In a bowl, mix together the egg yolks, sugar, and cornflour. Warm the milk in a heavy saucepan, then pour it into the egg yolk mixture, stirring constantly. Return the mixture to the pan and cook over a low heat, stirring constantly, until the custard thickens. Leave the custard to cool slightly.

5 Pour the custard over the sponges, fruit, and biscuits in the glass bowl. Cover the surface of the custard with a sheet of cling film, to prevent a skin from forming, and chill until set, preferably overnight (to let the sponge absorb the juices).

6 Whip the cream until thick and spread over the custard. Scatter the almonds over the top to decorate. Serve chilled.

BAILEYS AND CHOCOLATE TRIFLE

Replace the sherry with the same amount of Baileys cream liqueur. Grate 30g (1oz) dark chocolate over the pears once arranged. Replace the flaked almonds with 30g (1oz) grated dark chocolate or chocolate curls (page 195).

ORANGE ENGLISH TRIFLE

Omit the pears and flaked almonds. Use the orange segments from 2 large oranges and finely grate the zest (keep this for garnish). Replace the red jam with the same amount of apricot jam. Replace the sherry with the same amount of Grand Marnière. Continue with the recipe and garnish with orange zest instead of flaked almonds.

top: *Chocolate curls.*
bottom: *Fresh oranges.*

ZABAGLIONE

SERVES 6

4 egg yolks
75g (2½oz) caster sugar
125ml (4fl oz) Marsala or sweet sherry
savoiardi (Italian sponge fingers)
  or boudoir biscuits to serve

1 Whisk the egg yolks and sugar in a heatproof bowl until light and foamy. Add the Marsala, and whisk to blend.

2 Put the bowl over a pan of simmering water, making sure it does not touch the water. Heat gently, whisking the mixture until it becomes thick and creamy and stands in soft peaks.

3 Remove from the heat and whisk until cool. Pour into glass dishes and serve at once, with savoiardi.

Cook's know-how

Zabaglione is traditionally served warm, poured straight from the bowl into glass dishes as soon as it has thickened. This can be difficult if you are entertaining guests, which is why it is served cool in this recipe. Don't skimp on the whisking in step 3 or the mixture may separate.

AUSTRIAN CHEESECAKE

SERVES 8

20CM (8IN) LOOSE-BOTTOMED OR
  SPRINGFORM CAKE TIN

90g (3oz) butter, at room temperature,
  plus extra for greasing
150g (5oz) caster sugar
300g (10oz) curd cheese
2 eggs, separated
60g (2oz) ground almonds
2 tbsp semolina
grated zest and juice of 1 large lemon
60g (2oz) sultanas
icing sugar for dusting

1 Lightly butter the tin and line the bottom with a round of baking parchment.

2 Beat the butter with the sugar and curd cheese until light and creamy. Beat in the egg yolks, then stir in the almonds, semolina, and lemon zest and juice. Leave to stand for 10 minutes, then fold in the sultanas.

3 In a separate bowl, whisk the egg whites until stiff but not dry. Carefully fold into the cheese mixture.

4 Turn into the prepared tin and level the surface. Bake in a preheated oven at 190°C (375°F, Gas 5) for 30–35 minutes until browned and firm to the touch. Turn off the oven and leave the cheesecake inside to cool for about 1 hour. Chill before serving.

5 Use a knife to loosen the side of the cheesecake from the tin, then remove the cheesecake. Slide on to a serving plate, and dust with sifted icing sugar.

CRÈME BRÛLÉE

SERVES 6

6 SMALL RAMEKINS OR SHALLOW CRÈME BRÛLÉE DISHES

butter for greasing
4 egg yolks
30g (1oz) caster sugar
½ tsp vanilla extract
600ml (1 pint) single cream
60g (2oz) demerara sugar

1 Lightly butter the ramekins or crème brûlée dishes.

2 In a large bowl, beat the egg yolks with the caster sugar and vanilla extract. Heat the cream to just below boiling point, then slowly pour into the egg-yolk mixture, stirring all the time.

3 Carefully pour the custard into the ramekins or dishes. Set in a roasting tin and add enough hot water to come halfway up the sides of the ramekins or dishes.

4 Bake in a preheated oven at 160°C (325°F, Gas 3) for about 25 minutes, or until just set and firm to the touch. Leave to cool.

5 Sprinkle the demerara sugar evenly over the top of the set custard. Place under a very hot grill until the sugar melts and caramelizes to a rich golden brown colour.

6 Chill the crème brûlées for no more than 2 hours before serving.

Cook's know-how

The caramel topping should be hard and crisp; don't chill crème brûlée for too long, or the caramel will begin to soften. To reach the rich and creamy custard beneath, crack the hard caramel with the edge of a spoon.

CHOCOLATE ROULADE

SERVES 6

23 × 33CM (9 × 13IN) SWISS ROLL TIN

sunflower oil for greasing
175g (6oz) plain dark chocolate,
  broken into pieces
6 large eggs, separated
175g (6oz) caster sugar
icing sugar for dusting

FILLING

90g (3oz) plain dark chocolate,
  broken into pieces
300ml (½ pint) double or whipping cream,
  whipped until thick

1 Put the chocolate into a small heatproof bowl over a pan of hot water, stirring occasionally, to melt the chocolate. Cool. Whisk the egg yolks and sugar together in a large bowl until light and creamy. Add the cooled chocolate and blend evenly.

2 In a separate bowl, whisk the egg whites until stiff but not dry. Carefully fold into the chocolate mixture. Turn the mixture into the greased and lined tin, tilting the tin so that the mixture spreads evenly over the base. Bake in a preheated oven at 180°C (350°F, Gas 4) for 20 minutes or until firm to the touch.

3 Remove the tin from the oven. Place a clean, dry tea towel on top of the cake and on top of this lay another tea towel that has been soaked in cold water and wrung out. Leave in a cool place, for 8 hours.

4 Make the filling: put the chocolate into a heatproof bowl over a pan of hot water, stirring occasionally, to melt the chocolate. Cool. Remove the tea towels from the cake, and turn it out on to a sheet of baking parchment sprinkled with icing sugar. Peel the lining paper from the cake. Spread the chocolate over the cake, then spread the cream evenly over the top.

5 Roll up the cake from a long edge tightly at first, using the sugared paper to help lift the cake and roll it forward. Dust the roulade with more sifted icing sugar before serving.

SAUCES FOR DESSERTS

These sauces make a rich, flavourful accompaniment to plenty of desserts. Try the Hot Chocolate Sauce with chilled pears, the Chocolate Marshmallow Sauce with Meringue Raspberry Nests (page 176), Coffee and Almond Meringue Towers (page 178), and Chocolate Meringue Shells (page 180), the Butterscotch Sauce with Chocolate Profiteroles (page 234), Coffee Éclairs (page 236), and Religieuses (page 238), and the Peach Sauce with fresh raspberries and strawberries.

HOT CHOCOLATE

Put 175g (6oz) plain chocolate, broken into small pieces, 2 tsp instant coffee granules, 125ml (4fl oz) hot water, and 90g (3oz) caster sugar in a saucepan and heat gently until the chocolate has melted and the sugar and coffee granules has dissolved. Serve hot.

CHOCOLATE MARSHMALLOW

Put 60g (2oz) chopped plain chocolate into small pieces,100g (3½oz) marshmallows, 75ml (2½fl oz) double cream, and 75ml (2½fl oz) honey in a pan and heat until melted. Serve hot.

BUTTERSCOTCH

Heat 60g (2oz) butter, 150g (5oz) light muscovado sugar, and 150g (5oz) golden syrup in a pan until melted. Remove from the heat and add 150ml (¼ pint) double cream and ½ tsp vanilla extract, stirring constantly. Serve hot.

PEACH

Put 1 × 400g (13oz) can peaches and their juice into a food processor or blender with ¼ tsp almond extract. Work to a smooth purée. Serve chilled. Use fresh peaches instead, if desired, with a little sugar and some lemon juice.

Far right: A silky smooth chocolate sauce is a dessert staple. To save time, make a batch, chill, and reheat to serve.

CHOCOLATE DELICE

SERVES 6

125g (4oz) fresh brown breadcrumbs
90g (3oz) demerara sugar
75g (2½oz) drinking chocolate powder
2 tbsp instant coffee
300ml (½ pint) double cream
150ml (¼ pint) single cream
60g (2oz) plain dark chocolate, grated

1 In a bowl, mix together the breadcrumbs, sugar, drinking chocolate, and coffee granules. In another bowl, whip the creams together until they form soft peaks.

2 Spoon half of the cream into 6 glass serving dishes. Cover with the breadcrumb mixture and then with the remaining cream. Chill for at least 6 hours, or overnight for best results.

3 Sprinkle generously with the grated chocolate just before serving.

Cook's know-how
To make grating chocolate easy, chill it well in the refrigerator before you grate it, and use the largest holes on the grater.

CHOCOLATE-RUM MOUSSE

SERVES 6

250g (8oz) plain dark chocolate,
  broken into pieces
3 tbsp cold water
15g (½oz) powdered gelatine
4 eggs, plus 2 egg yolks
90g (3oz) caster sugar
3 tbsp dark rum
150ml (¼ pint) whipping cream,
  whipped until thick

DECORATION

150ml (¼ pint) double or whipping cream,
  whipped until stiff
chocolate curls or caraque (page 195)
  to decorate

1 Put the chocolate into a heatproof bowl over a pan of hot water. Heat gently until melted. Leave to cool.

2 Put the cold water into a heatproof bowl and sprinkle the gelatine over the top. Leave for about 10 minutes until spongy. Stand the bowl in a pan of hot water and heat gently until dissolved.

3 Combine the eggs, egg yolks, and sugar in a large heatproof bowl, and put over a saucepan of simmering water. Whisk with a hand-held electric mixer until the egg mixture is very thick and mousse-like. Whisk in the dissolved gelatine and rum.

4 Fold the whipped cream into the cooled chocolate, then fold into the egg mixture. Carefully pour into a glass serving bowl, cover, and leave in the refrigerator until set.

5 Decorate with piped rosettes of cream and chocolate curls or caraque (page 195). Serve the mousse chilled.

Cook's know-how

When melting chocolate in a bowl over hot water keep stirring as it melts. If the water boils the chocolate may become granular.

MOUSSE VARIATIONS

COFFEE-RUM MOUSSE
Omit the chocolate and replace the brandy with rum. Dissolve 2 tbsp of instant coffee in 3 tbsp of rum. Continue with the recipe.

WHITE CHOCOLATE AND BRANDY MOUSSE
Replace the dark chocolate with white chocolate and use the same method.

FRESH ORANGE MOUSSE
Omit the chocolate and replace with the finely grated zest and juice of 2 large oranges. Replace the water for soaking the gelatine with 3 tbsp fresh orange juice. Add the orange zest to the eggs and sugar before heating. Continue with the recipe.

clockwise from top left: *Coffee granules, white chocolate, and freshly squeezed orange juice.*

KEY TECHNIQUES

BASIC MERINGUE

Making meringue is a very easy process – the key is to incorporate plenty of air into the egg whites at the first stage. Although it is possible, whisking egg whites by hand takes a long time – an electric whisk is much more efficient. For best results use a very large bowl and move the whisk around the base of the bowl. Use this method when preparing Hazelnut Meringue Gâteau (page 182), Baked Alaska (page 196), Raspberry Meringue Roulade (page 204), and Stem Ginger and Pineapple Pavlova (page 206).

1 Whisk four egg whites in a scrupulously clean large bowl, with an electric mixer on maximum speed, until the whites are stiff and look like clouds.

2 Keeping the mixer on maximum speed, add 250g (8oz) caster sugar a teaspoon at a time and continue whisking until the mixture is stiff and shiny.

3 Pipe, spoon, or spread the meringue as preferred and bake as in the recipes above. All ovens vary, so baking times cannot be exact. You will know the meringues are cooked when they can be lifted easily from the parchment.

PIPING MERINGUE SHAPES

Made to the correct consistency, meringue is very easy and great fun to pipe. Try this technique to help prepare Meringue Raspberry Nests (page 176), Coffee and Almond Meringue Towers (page 178), and Chocolate Meringue Shells (page 180).

Nests

Mark 8 × 10cm (4in) circles on non-stick baking parchment; turn over. Spoon the meringue into a piping bag fitted with a medium star nozzle, and pipe inside the circles, building up the sides to form nests.

Shells

Spoon the meringue into a piping bag fitted with a medium star nozzle. Pipe 24 even-sized shells, about 5cm (2in) in diameter at the base, on to non-stick baking parchment.

MERINGUE RASPBERRY NESTS

MAKES 8

1 quantity basic meringue (page 174)
250ml (8fl oz) double cream
fresh raspberries and mint sprigs
  (optional) to decorate

RASPBERRY SAUCE

250g (8oz) fresh or frozen raspberries
2 tbsp icing sugar
a squeeze of lemon juice, to taste

1 Make the raspberry sauce: purée the raspberries in a blender or food processor, then push the purée through a sieve with a spoon into a bowl (discard the seeds in the sieve). Stir in the sugar and lemon juice to taste. Chill in the refrigerator until ready to use.

2 Pipe 8 meringue nests (see page 175). Bake in a preheated oven at 120°C (250°F, Gas ½) for 1–1½ hours until firm. Leave to cool.

3 Whip the cream until it forms stiff peaks. Fill the nests with the cream, top with berries, and decorate with mint sprigs if you like. Serve with the chilled raspberry sauce.

clockwise from top left: *Coffee and Almond Meringue Tower, Chocolate Meringue Shell, Meringue Raspberry Nest.*

COFFEE AND ALMOND MERINGUE TOWERS

MAKES 6

1 quantity basic meringue (page 174)
125g (4oz) slivered almonds
icing sugar for dusting

COFFEE CHANTILLY CREAM

250ml (8fl oz) double cream
1 tsp instant coffee, dissolved
   in 1 tbsp water
2–3 tbsp caster sugar

1 Spoon 18 mounds of meringue on to non-stick baking parchment, then spread them flat with a palette knife until they are very thin and about 7.5cm (3in) in diameter. Sprinkle over the almonds. Bake in a preheated oven at 120°C (250°F, Gas ½) for 1–1½ hours until firm. Cool.

2 Make the coffee Chantilly cream: whip the cream until it forms soft peaks. Add the coffee and sugar to the cream and whip until stiff peaks form.

3 Sandwich the meringue discs together in threes, with the coffee Chantilly cream in between. Dust with a little icing sugar before serving.

Illustrated on page 177.

Almonds work well with the coffee chantilly cream on this dessert.

CHOCOLATE MERINGUE SHELLS

MAKES 12

1 quantity basic meringue (page 174)
60g (2oz) plain chocolate, chopped

CHOCOLATE GANACHE

125g (4oz) plain chocolate, chopped
125ml (4fl oz) double cream

1 Pipe 24 shells (see page 175). Bake in a preheated oven at 120°C (250°F, Gas ½) for 1–1½ hours until firm. Leave to cool. Put the chocolate into a heatproof bowl over a pan of hot water and heat until melted. Drizzle over the meringues and leave to set.

2 Make the ganache: put the chopped chocolate and the cream into a heavy-based saucepan and heat gently, stirring occasionally, until the chocolate has melted.

3 Remove the pan from the heat. When the ganache is cool set and firm, sandwich the meringues together with the chocolate ganache.

Illustrated on page 177.

Buy a good quality plain dark chocolate. For the best flavour, look for a brand with at least 70 per cent cocoa solids.

SERVES 8

125g (4oz) shelled hazelnuts
4 egg whites
275g (9oz) caster sugar
300ml (½ pint) whipping cream,
   whipped until thick
icing sugar for dusting

RASPBERRY SAUCE

250g (8oz) raspberries
about 4 tbsp icing sugar, sifted

HAZELNUT MERINGUE GÂTEAU

1 Mark 2 × 20cm (8in) circles on 2 sheets of non-stick baking parchment. Turn the paper over and use to line 2 baking trays. Spread the hazelnuts on another baking tray and toast in a preheated oven at 190°C (375°F, Gas 5) for about 10 minutes. Remove from the oven, and adjust to 150°C (300°F, Gas 2).

2 Rub the nuts together inside a clean tea towel to remove the skins. Reserve 8 whole nuts for decoration and grind the remaining nuts in a food processor.

3 Whisk the egg whites on high speed until stiff but not dry. Add the caster sugar, 1 tsp at a time, and whisk until the sugar is incorporated and the mixture is stiff and glossy. Fold in the ground hazelnuts. Spread the mixture evenly over the two circles. Bake for an hour until the tops are crisp and pale beige in colour. Turn the oven off and leave the meringues inside for another hour. Lift off the baking trays, remove the paper, and cool on a wire rack.

4 Make the raspberry sauce: reserve 8 raspberries and blend the rest in a food processor, then sieve to remove the seeds. Whisk in the icing sugar to taste.

5 Use two-thirds of the whipping cream to sandwich the meringues together. Sift icing sugar over the top and decorate with rosettes (page 185) of remaining cream, topped with the reserved hazelnuts and raspberries. Serve with the raspberry sauce.

KEY TECHNIQUES

FILLING A PIPING BAG

Piped whipped cream adds a professional touch to desserts and cakes, and with a little practice and some confidence this is not difficult to do. A star-shaped nozzle is the most useful.

1 Drop the nozzle into the bag, then tuck the lower half of the bag into the nozzle, to stop the cream from leaking out when filling the bag.

2 Hold the bag in one hand, folding the top of the bag over your hand. Spoon in the whipped cream, trying not to create any air bubbles.

3 When the bag is full, twist the top until there is no air left. Pipe the cream as desired, gently squeezing the twisted end to force out the cream in a steady stream.

DECORATING WITH CREAM

Whipped cream can be piped to create many petterns. Here are just a few. Use this technique to decorate Chilled Lemon Soufflé (page 120), Hazelnut Meringue Gâteau (page 182), Chocolate Terrine (page 192), Chocolate and Orange Mousse Cake (page 224), White Chocolate Gâteau (page 228), Chocolate Profiteroles (page 234), Coffee Éclairs (page 236), and Religieuses (page 238).

Rosette
Hold the bag upright, just above the surface of the cake, squeeze gently, moving the bag in a small circle.

Swirl
Hold the bag upright, just above the surface of the cake. Squeeze the bag and pipe the cream to form an "S" shape.

Rope
Hold the bag at a 45° angle. Pipe a short length of cream to 1 side. Pipe another length of cream to the opposite side, overlapping the first one.

RICH VANILLA ICE CREAM

SERVES 4–6

4 egg yolks
125g (4oz) caster sugar
300ml (½ pint) milk
300ml (½pint) double cream
1½ tsp vanilla extract
strawberries to decorate

1 Put the egg yolks and sugar into a bowl and whisk until light in colour.

2 Heat the milk in a heavy pan to just below boiling point. Add a little of the hot milk to the egg-yolk mixture and stir to blend, then pour in the remaining milk.

3 Pour back into the pan and heat gently, stirring, until the froth disappears and the mixture coats the back of a spoon. Do not boil.

4 Leave the custard to cool, then stir in the cream and vanilla extract.

5 Pour into a container and freeze for 3 hours. Tip into a bowl and mash to break down the ice crystals. Return to container. Freeze for 2 hours. Mash and freeze for another 2 hours. Remove from the freezer 30 minutes before serving, and decorate.

VANILLA ICE CREAM VARIATIONS

CHOCOLATE ICE CREAM

In step 2, heat the milk with 125g (4oz) chopped dark chocolate. Let it melt before adding to the egg-yolk mixture.

CHOCOLATE CHIP ICE CREAM

In step 2, heat the milk with 125g (4oz) chopped white chocolate. Let it melt before adding to the egg-yolk mixture. Stir 60g (2oz) dark chocolate chips into the custard with the cream in step 4.

BANANA AND HONEY ICE CREAM

Mash 500g (1lb) bananas with 3 tbsp lemon juice and 2 tbsp honey. Add to the custard with the cream in step 4.

clockwise from top left: Dark chocolate, chocolate chips, and honey.

CASSATA

SERVES 8

900ML (1½ PINT) TERRINE OR LOAF TIN

30g (1oz) candied angelica, rinsed, dried, and chopped

30g (1oz) glacé cherries, rinsed, dried, and chopped

30g (1oz) chopped mixed candied peel

2 tbsp dark rum

600ml (1 pint) raspberry sorbet

150ml (¼ pint) double cream, whipped until thick

600ml (1 pint) vanilla ice cream

1 Chill the terrine. Put the angelica, glacé cherries, and candied peel in a bowl.

2 Add the rum and stir well, then leave to soak while preparing the ice-cream layers.

3 Allow the sorbet to soften, then spread it evenly over the bottom of the chilled terrine. Chill in the freezer until solid.

4 Fold the fruit and rum mixture into the whipped cream. Spoon into the terrine and level the surface. Return to the freezer until firm.

5 Allow the vanilla ice cream to soften, then spread it evenly over the fruit layer. Cover and freeze for 8 hours.

6 To turn out, dip the terrine into warm water and invert the cassata on to a large serving plate. Slice, and serve at once.

Cook's know-how

This is not a true cassata, but a layered ice-cream "sandwich" that has borrowed its name. A true Sicilian cassata is a bombe of liqueur-soaked sponge cake filled with ricotta cheese studded with candied fruits and grated chocolate. It is often served at wedding feasts and other celebrations.

SERVES 8–10

1KG (2LB) LOAF TIN

DARK CHOCOLATE LAYERS

250g (8oz) plain dark chocolate
2 tbsp brandy
2 eggs
375ml (13fl oz) double cream

WHITE CHOCOLATE LAYER

90g (3oz) white chocolate
1 egg
150ml (¼ pint) double cream

DECORATION

150ml (¼ pint) double or whipping
cream, whipped, grated chocolate,
and mint sprigs to decorate

CHOCOLATE TERRINE

1 Make the dark chocolate layers: break the dark chocolate into pieces and place in a heatproof bowl with the brandy over a pan of hot water. Heat gently to melt, then leave to cool.

2 Line the loaf tin with cling film. Set aside. Put the eggs into a heatproof bowl over a pan of hot water. Whisk until the eggs are thick and mousse-like, and leave a trail when the whisk is lifted. Remove from the heat and whisk until the bowl is completely cold.

3 Whip the cream until it just holds its shape. Fold the whisked eggs into the cooled chocolate mixture, then fold in the cream.

4 Pour half of the dark chocolate mixture into the prepared tin, then freeze for about 15 minutes until firm. Reserve the remaining dark chocolate mixture.

5 Meanwhile, make the white chocolate mixture in the same way as the dark chocolate mixture. Pour the white chocolate mixture on top of the firm layer in the tin, and freeze for 15 minutes.

6 Spoon the reserved dark chocolate mixture onto the white chocolate layer and freeze for 30 minutes.

7 Invert the tin on to a serving plate, and remove the cling film. Decorate the terrine with piped rosettes of whipped cream (page 185), grated chocolate, and mint sprigs. Slice thinly to serve.

KEY TECHNIQUES

MELTING CHOCOLATE

Care is needed when melting chocolate, especially white chocolate. Don't allow it to overheat or come into contact with any steam as this could cause it to scorch or harden. Use this technique when making Magic Chocolate Pudding (page 96), Chocolate Roulade (page 164), Chocolate-rum Mousse (page 170), Chocolate Terrine (page 192), Heavenly Chocolate cake (page 214), and Chocolate and Orange Mousse Cake (page 224).

Heating chocolate
Chop the chocolate and put it into a heatproof bowl set over a pan of hot, not boiling, water. The base of the bowl should not be touching the water. Heat gently, without stirring, until the chocolate becomes soft. Remove from the heat, but leave the bowl over the water. Stir until the chocolate is very smooth and creamy.

DECORATING WITH CHOCOLATE

Chocolate decorations can transform a dessert, and you don't have to reserve them for desserts made only from chocolate – fruit fools and mousses can also benefit from a contrasting finishing touch.

Grating chocolate
Use chilled chocolate and hold it firmly in a piece of greaseproof paper. Hold the grater on a sheet of greaseproof paper and rub the chocolate over the large grid of the grater.

Chocolate curls
Have the chocolate at room temperature, and use a vegetable peeler to shave off long curls on to a sheet of greaseproof paper. Lift the paper to tip the curls on to the dessert.

Chocolate caraque
1 Spread a smooth, thin layer of melted chocolate, about 1.5mm (1/16in) thick, on to a cool work surface, and leave to cool until nearly set.

2 Using a long, sharp knife held at an angle, push across the chocolate with a slight sawing action, to shave it into "caraque" curls. Use a cocktail stick to pick up the caraque.

BAKED ALASKA

SERVES 8

1 × 20CM (8IN) SPONGE FLAN CASE

250g (8oz) raspberries, sliced
  strawberries, or other summer fruits
450ml (¾ pint) vanilla ice cream
2 egg whites
125g (4oz) caster sugar
whole berries to decorate

1 Put the sponge flan case into a shallow ovenproof serving dish. Arrange the fruits in the case.

2 Put the ice cream on top of the fruits and put in the freezer to keep the ice cream frozen while making the meringue.

3 Whisk the egg whites (an electric mixer can be used) until stiff but not dry.

4 Add the caster sugar, 1 tsp at a time, and continue to whisk until the sugar has been incorporated and the meringue mixture is stiff and glossy.

5 Pipe or spoon the meringue over the ice cream, covering it completely.

6 Bake immediately in a preheated oven at 230°C (450°F, Gas 8) for 3–4 minutes until the meringue is tinged with brown. Serve at once, decorated with raspberries and strawberries.

Cook's know-how

A block of firm ice cream is needed for this recipe – do not use soft-scoop ice cream. Make sure the ice cream is completely covered by the egg white, which stops the ice cream melting.

SERVES 8

1.75 LITRE (3 PINT) PUDDING BOWL

175g (6oz) mixed dried fruit
60g (2oz) ready-to-eat dried
  apricots, chopped
60g (2oz) glacé cherries, halved
3 tbsp brandy

ICE CREAM

3 eggs
125g (4oz) caster sugar
450ml (¾ pint) milk
450ml (¾ pint) double cream
150ml (¼ pint) single cream

ICED CHRISTMAS PUDDING

1 Combine the dried fruit, apricots, glacé cherries, and brandy. Cover and leave to soak for 8 hours.

2 In a large bowl, whisk together the eggs and sugar. Heat the milk in a heavy saucepan to just below boiling point. Pour into the egg mixture, stirring.

3 Pour back into the pan. Cook gently, stirring with a wooden spoon, until the froth disappears and the mixture thickens. Do not boil. Remove from the heat and leave to cool.

4 Whip 300ml (½ pint) double cream and the single cream together until they are just beginning to hold their shape. Fold into the custard with the fruit and brandy mixture.

5 Turn into a shallow freezerproof container and freeze for 2 hours or until beginning to set but still slightly soft.

6 Remove the soft set mixture from the freezer and mix well to distribute the fruit evenly. Spoon into the pudding bowl, cover, and return to the freezer. Freeze for 6 hours or until firm.

7 Remove from the freezer about 20 minutes before serving to soften. Turn out on to a serving plate, and spoon the remaining cream, lightly whipped, on top. Slice and serve at once.

SERVES 8

125ml (4fl oz) strong coffee
3 tbsp brandy
2 eggs
65g (2½oz) light muscovado sugar
250g (8oz) mascarpone cheese
300ml (½ pint) double cream,
  whipped until thick
1 packet trifle sponges
60g (2oz) plain dark chocolate,
  coarsely grated
30g (1oz) white chocolate, coarsely
  grated, to decorate

DIVINE TIRAMISU

1 Mix the coffee and brandy together.

2 Combine the eggs and caster sugar in a large bowl and whisk together until thick and light, and the mixture leaves a trail on the surface.

3 Put the mascarpone into a bowl and stir in a little of the egg mixture. Fold in the rest, then fold in the cream.

4 Cut the trifle sponges horizontally in half. Line the bottom of a large glass serving bowl with half of the sponge pieces. Drizzle half of the coffee and brandy mixture over the sponges. Spread half the mascarpone mixture over the top, and scatter half the plain chocolate over the marscapone.

5 Repeat the layers with the remaining ingredients, decorating the top with the grated white chocolate and the remaining grated plain chocolate. Cover and chill for at least 4 hours before serving.

LUXURY CRÈME CARAMEL

SERVES 6

6 SMALL RAMEKINS

175g (6oz) granulated sugar
8 tbsp water
4 eggs
30g (1oz) vanilla sugar (see box, below)
150ml (¼ pint) double cream
450ml (¾ pint) milk

1 Combine the sugar and water in a saucepan and heat gently until all the sugar has dissolved. Bring to a boil, and cook without stirring, until pale golden. Pour into the ramekins.

2 Whisk the eggs and vanilla sugar in a bowl. Heat the milk and cream until warm, then pour into the egg mixture, stirring well. Strain into the ramekins.

3 Put the ramekins in a roasting tin and add enough hot water to come halfway up the sides of the ramekins. Bake in a preheated oven at 160°C (325°F, Gas 3) for about 40 minutes until just set and firm to the touch but not solid. Cool, then chill for 8 hours.

4 Turn out on to individual plates to serve.

Cook's know-how

You can buy sachets of vanilla sugar or make your own by pushing a halved vanilla pod into a jar of caster sugar – after a few days the sugar will smell and taste of vanilla. If you don't have vanilla sugar, use caster sugar and 1 tsp vanilla extract.

RASPBERRY MERINGUE ROULADE

SERVES 8

23 × 33CM (9 × 13IN) SWISS ROLL TIN

butter for greasing
4 egg whites
250g (8oz) caster sugar
45g (1^{1}/$_{2}$oz) flaked almonds
icing sugar for dusting

FILLING

300ml (^{1}/$_{2}$ pint) double or whipping
   cream, whipped until thick
250g (8oz) raspberries
strawberries to garnish

1 Lightly butter the Swiss roll tin and line with a sheet of baking parchment.

2 Whisk the egg whites on full speed until stiff but not dry. Add the sugar, 1 tsp at a time, and continue to whisk, still at full speed, until all the sugar has been incorporated and the mixture is stiff and glossy.

3 Spoon the meringue into the lined tin and spread to level the surface. Sprinkle over the flaked almonds.

4 Bake low down in a preheated oven at 200°C (400°F, Gas 6) for about 8 minutes until the top is golden brown. Make sure it doesn't burn.

5 Reduce the oven temperature to 160°C (325°F, Gas 3), and continue baking for 10 minutes or until the meringue is firm to the touch.

6 Remove the meringue from the oven and turn out on to a sheet of baking parchment. Peel the lining paper from the base and leave to cool for 10 minutes.

7 Spread the whipped cream evenly over the meringue, and scatter the raspberries over the cream.

8 Roll up the meringue from a long side, using the lining paper to help lift it. Wrap the roulade in baking parchment and chill in the refrigerator for 30 minutes. Lightly dust with sifted icing sugar before serving.

STEM GINGER AND PINEAPPLE PAVLOVA

SERVES 6–8

4 egg whites
250g (8oz) caster sugar
1½ tsp cornflour
1½ tsp white wine vinegar

TOPPING

375ml (13fl oz) double or whipping cream
60g (2oz) stem ginger in syrup, cut into
 matchstick-thin strips
1 × 400g (13oz) can pineapple
 rings, drained, or freshly cut pineapple

1 Preheat the oven to 160°C (325°F, Gas 3). Mark a 23cm (9in) circle on a sheet of non-stick baking parchment, turn the paper over, and line a baking tray.

2 Whisk the egg whites on full speed until stiff, then add the sugar, 1 tsp at a time, whisking the mixture constantly on full speed.

3 Blend the cornflour and vinegar and whisk into the egg white mixture.

4 Spread the mixture inside the circle on the baking parchment, building the sides up so that they are higher than the middle. Place in the oven, then immediately reduce the heat to 150°C (300°F, Gas 2).

5 Bake the meringue for 1 hour or until firm to the touch. Turn off the oven and leave the meringue inside for another hour.

6 Peel the lining paper from the meringue, and transfer to a serving plate. Leave to cool.

7 Before serving, whip the cream until stiff, and stir in half of the stem ginger strips. Spoon the mixture into the middle of the meringue. Top with the pineapple rings and the remaining stem ginger strips.

PEAR AND GINGER

Replace the pineapple with 1 x 400g (13oz) can pears. Continue with the recipe.

MINT AND CHOCOLATE

Omit the pineapple and ginger. Crush 225g (8oz) mint and ginger chocolates into small pieces. Mix into the whipped cream and add 1 tsp peppermint extract. Garnish with shavings of dark chocolate and fresh mint leaves.

TRIPLE BERRY PAVLOVA

Omit the pineapple and ginger. Replace with 250g (5oz) fresh blueberries, 200g (7oz) fresh raspberries and 200g (7oz) fresh strawberries, quartered. Stir half of each fruit into the whipped cream and scatter the remainder over the top.

BANOFFE PAVLOVA

Omit the pineapple and ginger. Add to large bananas to the whipped cream and stir in 3 tbsp of toffee sauce from a jar. Garnish with shaving of chocolate.

clockwise from top left: *Pears, mint leaves, mixed berries, and bananas.*

LEMON PANNACOTTA

SERVES 8

8 INDIVIDUAL GLASS DISHES OR RAMEKINS

2 tbsp cold water
1 x 11g packet powdered gelatine
750ml (1¼ pint) single cream
75g (3oz) caster sugar
grated rind and juice of 1 lemon
blueberries and redcurrants to garnish

1 Measure the cold water into a small container and sprinkle the gelatine over evenly. Set aside to sponge.

2 Measure the cream, sugar, and lemon rind into a saucepan and bring the cream to scalding point (just below boiling), stir to dissolve the sugar. Remove from the heat and cool very slightly. Add gelatine in a "lump" and whisk until dissolved and smooth. Add the lemon juice. Pour into glass dishes and allow to set in the refrigerator, for about 6 hours or, ideally, overnight. If you prefer not to have the lemon rind, strain the mixture strain after heating.

3 Serve straight from the refrigerator, turned out onto individual serving plates and garnish with the blueberries and redcurrants.

Dessert Cakes

HEAVENLY CHOCOLATE CAKE

CUTS INTO 8 SLICES

DEEP 20CM (8IN) CAKE TIN

125g (4oz) butter, plus extra for greasing
200g (7oz) plain dark chocolate,
    broken into pieces
2 tbsp water
3 eggs, separated
125g (4oz) caster sugar
90g (3oz) self-raising flour
60g (2oz) ground almonds

FUDGE ICING

60g (2oz) butter
30g (1oz) cocoa powder
3 tbsp milk
250g (8oz) icing sugar, sifted
white chocolate curls (page 195)
    to decorate

1 Lightly butter the tin and line the bottom with baking parchment.

2 Put the chocolate into a heatproof bowl with the butter and water. Put the bowl over a pan of hot water and heat gently, stirring, until the mixture has melted. Cool.

3 Whisk the egg yolks and caster sugar together with an electric whisk in a large bowl until fluffy and very light in colour. Stir in the cooled chocolate mixture. Carefully fold in the flour and ground almonds.

4 In a separate bowl, whisk the egg whites until stiff but not dry. Fold into the sponge mixture, gently but thoroughly. Pour the mixture into the prepared tin. Bake in a preheated oven at 180°C (350°F, Gas 4) for 50 minutes or until well risen and firm to the touch.

5 Leave the cake to cool in the tin for a few minutes, turn out on to a wire rack, and peel off the lining paper. Cool completely. Make the fudge icing: melt the butter in a pan, add the cocoa powder, and cook, stirring, for 1 minute. Stir in the milk and icing sugar. Beat well until smooth. Leave to cool until thickened.

6 Split the cake in half horizontally and sandwich the layers together with half of the fudge icing. With a palette knife, spread the remaining icing over the cake. Decorate with white chocolate curls.

KEY TECHNIQUES

WHISKED CAKES

Light, fatless sponges are raised by air whisked into eggs. Use a hand-held electric mixer or a large, table-top mixer. If using a hand-held mixer, set it at high speed.

1 Whisk the eggs, or egg yolks, with the sugar until the mixture is light, pale, and thick enough to leave a trail on the surface when the beaters are lifted out.

2 Gently fold in the flour and any other ingredients. If the eggs have been separated, the whisked egg whites should be folded into the mixture last of all with a spatula.

CREAMED CAKES

The creaming method is used for both cakes and biscuits. A wooden spoon, rubber spatula, or electric mixer are all suitable. Be sure to soften the butter or margarine first. Use this method when preparing Devil's Food Cake (page 220).

1 With a wooden spoon, cream the fat and sugar together until the mixture is pale in colour and fluffy in texture. Keep scraping the side of the bowl with a spoon or spatula to incorporate all of the mixture.

2 Lightly beat the eggs. Gradually add the eggs to the creamed mixture, beating well until smooth between each addition. If the mixture curdles, which will result in a dense-textured cake, beat in a spoonful of the flour.

3 Sift over the flour and any other dry ingredients. Using a wooden spoon, gently fold until well combined. Any liquid ingredients should also be added at this stage.

CARROT CAKE

CUTS INTO 10 SQUARES

18CM (7IN) SQUARE CAKE TIN

150ml (¼ pint) sunflower oil,
   plus extra for greasing
250g (8oz) wholemeal self-raising flour
2 tsp baking powder
150g (5oz) light muscovado sugar
60g (2oz) walnuts, coarsely chopped
125g (4oz) carrots, grated
2 ripe bananas, mashed
2 eggs
1 tbsp milk

TOPPING

250g (8oz) low-fat soft cheese,
   at room temperature
2 tsp clear honey
1 tsp lemon juice
chopped walnuts to decorate

1 Lightly grease the cake tin and line the bottom with baking parchment.

2 Combine all the cake ingredients in a large bowl. Mix well until thoroughly blended. Turn into the prepared cake tin and level the surface.

3 Bake in a preheated oven at 180°C (350°F, Gas 4) for about 50 minutes until the cake is well risen, firm to the touch, and beginning to shrink away from the sides of the tin.

4 Leave the cake to cool in the tin for a few minutes. Turn out on to a wire rack, peel off the lining paper, and leave to cool completely.

5 Make the topping: mix together the cheese, honey, and lemon juice. Spread on top of the cake and sprinkle the walnuts over the top. Store the cake in the refrigerator until ready to serve.

Healthy option

A full-fat cream cheese frosting is the traditional topping for carrot cake, but here a low-fat soft cheese is suggested, and it tastes equally good. If you prefer not to have frosting at all, spread clear honey on top of the cake while it is hot from the oven, and sprinkle with chopped walnuts.

DEVIL'S FOOD CAKE

CUTS INTO 12 SLICES

3 × 20CM (8IN) SANDWICH CAKE TINS

175g (6oz) soft butter, plus extra
for greasing
90g (3oz) plain dark chocolate,
broken into pieces
175ml (6fl oz) hot water
300g (10oz) light muscovado sugar
3 eggs, beaten
300g (10oz) plain flour
1½ tsp bicarbonate of soda
1½ tsp baking powder
1 tsp vanilla extract
150ml (¼ pint) soured cream

AMERICAN FROSTING

400g (13oz) caster sugar
2 egg whites
4 tbsp hot water
pinch of cream of tartar

1 Grease the tins with butter and line the bottoms with baking parchment.

2 Put the chocolate into a pan with the water. Heat gently, stirring, until the chocolate melts. Cool.

3 Combine the butter and sugar in a bowl and beat until light and fluffy. Gradually beat in the eggs.

4 Stir in the melted chocolate. Sift together the flour, bicarbonate of soda, and baking powder. Fold into the chocolate mixture until evenly blended, then fold in the vanilla essence and soured cream.

5 Divide the mixture evenly among the prepared tins. Bake in a preheated oven at 190°C (375°F, Gas 5) for 25 minutes until well risen, springy to the touch, and just shrinking in from the tin's sides.

6 Turn out the cakes on to a wire rack, peel off the lining paper, and leave to cool.

7 Make the American frosting: combine all the ingredients in a heatproof bowl. Set the bowl over a pan of hot water and whisk with an electric mixer for 12 minutes or until the mixture is white, thick, and stands in peaks.

8 Use half of the American frosting to sandwich the layers together, then spread the remainder over the top and side of the cake, swirling it decoratively and pulling it into peaks with the flat of a palette knife.

KEY TECHNIQUES

PREPARING CAKE TINS

Lightly greasing the tin ensures a cake will turn out easily. Some recipes, such as Heavenly Chocolate Cake (page 214), Carrot Cake (page 218), Devil's Food Cake (page 220), Chocolate and Orange Mousse Cake (page 224), White Chocolate Gâteau (page 228), and Iced Lime Traybake (page 240), call for the tin to be floured or lined with greaseproof paper or baking parchment.

Greasing and flouring

Use melted or softened butter or margarine, or oil, according to the recipe. Brush over the bottom and side of the tin using a pastry brush or paper towels. If flouring, add a spoonful of flour and tilt the tin to coat it with a thin layer. Tip out any excess flour.

Lining

1 Set the cake tin on a sheet of greaseproof paper or baking parchment. Holding the tin steady with one hand, mark around the base with a pencil or the tip of a knife with the other hand.

2 Cut out the shape, cutting just inside the line, so that no trace of the lead gets into the cake, then press smoothly over the bottom of the tin. Lightly grease if directed in the recipe. This will allow the cake to easily fall out of the tin.

BAKING SUCCESS

It can be very dis-heartening when cakes don't turn out right after you've spent time carefully weighing ingredients and baking them. Follow these simple rules to produce a perfect cake every time:

Be sure to use the correct size tin, as stated in the recipe. To check the dimensions of a cake tin, measure inside the top rim. To work out the depth, measure from the bottom to the top rim on the inside of the tin. To check the capacity of a tin, measure how much water is needed to fill it to the brim.

When measuring ingredients with a spoon, don't hold the spoon directly over the bowl or you may accidentally add too much.

If baking several cake layers, stagger them on the oven shelves so one is not directly beneath another.

Bake for the minimum time given in the recipe before opening the oven door. If the door is opened too soon it may cause some cakes to deflate.

If a cake looks as though it is browning too quickly, cover the top loosely with foil.

CHOCOLATE AND ORANGE MOUSSE CAKE

CUTS INTO 12 SLICES

DEEP 23CM (9IN) SPRINGFORM CAKE TIN

butter for greasing
4 eggs
125g (4oz) caster sugar
90g (3oz) self-raising flour
30g (1oz) cocoa powder

MOUSSE

175g (6oz) plain dark chocolate,
   broken into pieces
grated zest and juice of 1 orange
1 tsp powdered gelatine
2 eggs, separated
300ml (½ pint) double cream,
   whipped until thick

DECORATION

300ml (½ pint) double or whipping
   cream, whipped until thick
strips of orange zest, blanched

1 Lightly butter the tin and line the bottom with baking parchment. Make the sponge (page 226).

2 Bake the sponge in a preheated oven at 180°C (350°F, Gas 4) for 40–45 minutes until the sponge is well risen. Turn out on to a wire rack, peel off the lining paper, and leave to cool. Cut the cake in half horizontally. Put one half back into the clean tin.

4 Make the mousse: put the chocolate into a bowl set over a pan of hot water. Heat gently, stirring occasionally, until the chocolate has melted.

5 While the chocolate cools, strain the orange juice into a small bowl and sprinkle over the gelatine. Leave for 3 minutes or until spongy, then stand the bowl in a saucepan of gently simmering water for 3 minutes or until the gelatine has dissolved.

6 Stir the egg yolks and orange zest into the cooled chocolate. Slowly stir in the gelatine, then fold in the whipped cream. In a separate bowl, whisk the egg whites until stiff, then fold into the chocolate mixture.

7 Pour the mousse on top of the cake layer in the tin. Put the remaining cake layer on top. Cover and chill until the mousse is set.

8 Remove the side of the tin and slide the cake on to a serving plate. Decorate with cream and orange zest.

KEY TECHNIQUES

MAKING A FATLESS SPONGE

Sponge can be deliciously soft and moist. The key to achieving this is to whisk the eggs and sugar to the correct stage in the first step. For the quantities referred to in this recipe see the Chocolate and Orange Mousse Cake (page 224). These instructions will also help you to make White Chocolate Gâteau (page 228).

1 Combine the eggs and sugar in a large bowl and whisk with an electric mixer at high speed until the mixture is pale and thick enough to leave a trail on itself.

2 Sift the flour and cocoa powder together over the surface. Don't be tempted to use drinking chocolate powder, as it is too sweet and weak in flavour.

Far right: Whisk with an electric whisk on full speed until the mixture becomes smooth, not textured.

3 Fold in the flour and cocoa with a plastic spatula until fully blended.

4 Turn the mixture into the prepared tin and tilt to level the surface.

WHITE CHOCOLATE GÂTEAU

CUTS INTO 14 SLICES

DEEP 23CM (9IN) ROUND CAKE TIN

90g (3oz) butter, melted and cooled
  slightly, plus extra for greasing
6 large eggs
175g (6oz) caster sugar
125g (4oz) self-raising flour
30g (1oz) cocoa powder
2 tbsp cornflour

FILLING AND TOPPING

300ml (½ pint) double or whipping
  cream, whipped until thick
white chocolate curls
  (optional – page 195)

1 Lightly butter the cake tin and line the bottom of the tin with baking parchment.

2 Put the eggs and sugar into a large bowl and whisk together with an electric mixer on high speed until the mixture is pale and thick enough to leave a trail on itself when the whisk is lifted out.

3 Sift together the flour, cocoa powder, and cornflour, and fold half into the egg mixture. Pour half of the cooled butter around the edge; fold in gently.

4 Repeat with the remaining flour mixture and butter, folding gently.

5 Turn the mixture into the prepared cake tin and tilt the tin to level the surface. Bake in a preheated oven at 180°C (350°F, Gas 4) for 35–40 minutes until the sponge is well risen and firm to the touch. Turn out on to a rack, peel off the lining, and cool.

6 Cut the cake in half horizontally and sandwich the layers together with half of the whipped cream. Cover the cake with a thin layer of cream, then pipe the remainder around the top and bottom edges.

7 Press the chocolate curls over the top and side of the cake, if preferred.

KEY TECHNIQUES

BAKING AND TESTING

It is important to test cakes, teabreads, and biscuits before you remove them from the oven. Before baking, be sure to preheat the oven to the correct temperature. If you need to, adjust the position of the shelves before you turn on the oven. Use these techniques when making Heavenly Chocolate Cake (page 214), Carrot Cake (page 218), Devil's Food Cake (page 220), Chocolate and Orange Mousse Cake (page 224), and White Chocolate Gâteau (page 228).

1 Once prepared, turn the mixture into the tin and level the surface. Tap on the work surface to break any large air bubbles. Transfer to the oven.

2 When cooked, a cake will shrink slightly from the side of the tin. To test, lightly press the middle with a fingertip; the cake should spring back.

3 Set the cake tin on a wire rack and leave to cool for about 10 minutes. Run a knife around the side of the cake to free it from the tin.

COOLING AND CUTTING

Leave cakes to cool in the tin a little before turning out. It is best to turn out when they are luke warm, not completely cool. Leave to become stone cold on a cooling rack, before cutting and icing.

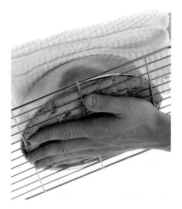

1 Hold a wire rack over the top of the tin, then invert the rack and tin so that the cake falls on to the rack. Carefully lift the tin away from the cake.

2 Peel off the lining paper. With a light-textured cake, turn it over again so the base is on the rack; this will prevent the rack marking the top.

3 To cut the cake in half, steady it by setting one hand gently on top. Cut the cake horizontally, using a gentle sawing action.

KEY TECHNIQUES

BASIC CHOUX PASTRY

Quite unlike any other pastry, choux is a thick paste that can be piped into any shape you like. Once baked, the light-as-air pastry literally melts in the mouth when it's packed with a creamy filling and topped with icing. Use this technique to make Chocolate Profiteroles (page 234), Coffee Éclairs (page 236), and Religieuses (page 238).

1 Put 60g (2oz) butter, cut into cubes, into a heavy saucepan with 150ml (¼ pint) water and heat over a medium heat for about 10 minutes or until the butter melts. Bring to a boil but take care not to burn the butter.

2 Take the saucepan off the heat and add 75g (2½oz) sifted plain flour. Stir vigorously with a wooden spoon until the mixture forms a soft ball. This should take around 3 minutes.

3 Leave to cool slightly, then gradually add 2 lightly beaten eggs, beating well between each addition, to form a smooth, shiny paste.

CRÈME PÂTISSIÈRE

The velvety texture of crème pâtissière, or pastry cream, is light and moreish when partnered with pastry. As well as using this recipe with the Mille-feuille (page 44), you could also try it with Chocolate Profiterles (page 234), Coffee Éclairs (page 236), and Religieuses (page 238). For the best taste make crème pâtissière just before you intend to serve it.

1 Put 3 eggs, 90g (3oz) caster sugar, 1½ tsp vanilla extract, and 60g (2oz) plain flour into a bowl, add a little milk taken from 400ml (14fl oz), and mix until smooth. Pour the rest of the milk into a heavy saucepan and bring almost to a boil.

2 Pour the hot milk on to the egg mixture, whisking well. Rinse out the saucepan to remove any milk residue. Return the egg mixture to the pan, and cook over a gentle heat, stirring continuously, until thickened.

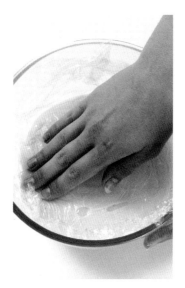

3 Pour into a bowl and cover with cling film, gently pressing it over the surface of the custard to prevent a skin from forming. Leave to cool.

CHOCOLATE PROFITEROLES

MAKES 12

butter for greasing
1 quantity choux pastry (page 232)
300ml (½ pint) whipping cream, whipped
1 quantity warm Wicked Chocolate Icing
(page 238)

1 Butter a baking tray and sprinkle with water. Put 12 tablespoonfuls of choux on the tray. Bake in a preheated oven at 220°C (425°F, Gas 7) for 10 minutes, then reduce the heat to 190°C (375°F, Gas 5) and bake for 20 minutes. Split each profiterole in half and cool on a rack.

2 Make the wicked chocolate icing (page 238).

3 Sandwich the profiteroles together with the whipped cream, place on individual plates, and drizzle with the chocolate icing.

clockwise from top left: *Coffee Éclairs, Religieuses, Chocolate Profiteroles.*

COFFEE ÉCLAIRS

MAKES 10–12

butter for greasing
1 quantity choux pastry (page 232)
300ml (½ pint) whipping cream, whipped

COFFEE ICING

1 tsp instant coffee
15g (½oz) butter
2 tbsp water
90g (3oz) icing sugar

1 Butter a baking tray and sprinkle with water. Spoon the choux into a piping bag fitted with a 1cm (½in) plain nozzle and pipe into 7cm (3in) lengths. Bake in a preheated oven at 220°C (425°F, Gas 7) for 10 minutes, then bake at 190°C (375°F, Gas 5) for 20 minutes. Split in half and cool on a rack.

2 Spoon the whipped cream into the bottom halves of the éclairs.

3 Make the icing: put the coffee, butter, and water in a bowl over a pan of water. Heat gently until the butter melts. Remove from the heat and beat in the icing sugar until it reaches spreading consistency. Dip the top half of each éclair in the coffee icing, then place on top of the cream. Leave the icing to cool before serving.

Illustrated on page 235.

The taste of rich aromatic coffee is as satisfying in a dessert as it is in a drink.

RELIGIEUSES

MAKES 10

butter for greasing
1 quantity choux pastry (page 232)
300ml (¹/₂ pint) whipping cream, whipped

WICKED CHOCOLATE ICING

150g (5oz) plain chocolate, chopped
150ml (¹/₄ pint) double cream

1 Butter a baking tray and sprinkle with water. Spoon the choux into a piping bag fitted with a 1cm (¹/₂in) plain nozzle and pipe 10 small and 10 slightly larger balls. Bake in a preheated oven at 220°C (425°F, Gas 7) for 10 minutes, then bake at 190°C (375°F, Gas 5) for 20 minutes. Split one side of each bun and cool on a rack.

2 Reserve about 3 tbsp of the whipped cream. Fill the balls with the remaining whipped cream, spooning it in the sides.

3 Make the wicked chocolate icing: gently melt the chocolate with the double cream in a bowl over a pan of simmering water, stirring until smooth and shiny (take care not to let it get too hot).

4 Dip the tops of a large and small ball in the icing. Fit a piping bag with a 1cm (¹/₂in) star nozzle and pipe the reserved cream on top of the large ball (see page 184). Gently press the small ball on top of the cream, with the icing facing up. Repeat with the other balls.

Illustrated on page 235.

Heating chocolate gently over simmering water is the ideal way to melt it.

MAKES 12 SQUARES

23 × 30CM (9 × 12IN) CAKE TIN

175g (6oz) soft butter or margarine,
  plus extra for greasing
175g (6oz) caster sugar
250g (8oz) self-raising flour
1 tsp baking powder
3 eggs
3 tbsp milk
finely grated zest of 2 limes

ICING

250g (8oz) icing sugar
juice of 2 limes

ICED LIME TRAYBAKE

1 Lightly grease the tin and line the bottom with baking parchment.

2 Combine all the cake ingredients in a large bowl and beat well for about 2 minutes or until smooth and thoroughly blended.

3 Turn into the prepared tin and level the surface. Bake in a preheated oven at 180°C (350°F, Gas 4) for 35–40 minutes until the cake is well risen, springy to the touch, and beginning to shrink away from the sides of the cake tin.

4 Leave to cool slightly in the tin, then turn out on to a wire rack, peel off the lining paper, and cool.

5 Make the icing: sift the icing sugar into a bowl. Mix in enough of the lime juice to give a runny consistency. Pour over the cooled cake, spreading carefully with a palette knife, and leave to set. When cold, cut into squares and serve.

MARBLED COFFEE RING CAKE

CUTS INTO 12 SLICES

1.75 LITRE (2¾ PINT) RING MOULD

250g (8oz) soft butter, plus extra
    for greasing
250g (8oz) caster sugar
4 eggs
250g (8oz) self-raising flour
2 tsp baking powder
2 tsp instant coffee
1 tbsp hot water
30g (1oz) white chocolate

ICING

60g (2oz) butter, softened
3 tbsp milk
2 tbsp instant coffee
250g (8oz) icing sugar, sifted

1 Lightly grease the ring mould with butter.

2 Combine the butter, sugar, eggs, flour, and baking powder in a large bowl. Beat until smooth.

3 Put half of the mixture into another bowl. Dissolve the instant coffee in the measured hot water and stir into one half of the cake mixture.

4 Drop tablespoonfuls of the plain mixture into the ring mould, then drop tablespoonfuls of the coffee mixture over it. Swirl with a skewer to marble.

5 Bake in a preheated oven at 180°C (350°F, Gas 4) for 40 minutes or until well risen and firm to the touch. Leave to cool for a few minutes, then turn out on to a wire rack set over a tray, and cool completely.

6 Make the icing: combine the butter, milk, and coffee in a pan and heat, stirring, until smooth. Remove from the heat and beat in the icing sugar until smooth and glossy.

7 Leave to cool, then pour over the cake, spreading it over the sides to cover completely. Leave to set.

8 Melt the white chocolate in a heatproof bowl over a pan of hot water. Cool slightly, then spoon into a clean plastic bag. Snip off a corner of the bag and drizzle the chocolate over the cake. Leave to set.

KEY TECHNIQUES

MAKING BUTTER ICING

There are many simple ways to fill or decorate cakes. Whipped cream, jam, or chocolate spread make quick and easy fillings. Butter-icing can be made in a variety of flavours, to complement the flavour of the cake.

Chocolate butter-icing
In a bowl, soften 150g (5oz) butter. Add 30g (1oz) cocoa powder and 250g (8oz) sifted icing sugar, and beat together until smooth. Add a little milk if necessary to give a spreading consistency. For a citrus icing, omit the cocoa powder and add finely grated orange or lemon zest.

ICING A CAKE

Spreading icing evenly over a cake creates an attractive surface that you can then decorate with anything – from whipped cream to holly. Use this technique to ice Heavenly Chocolate Cake (page 214), Carrot Cake (page 218), Devil's Food Cake (page 220), and Iced Lime Traybake (page 240).

Spreading the icing
Only ice a cake when it has cooled completely. Use a large palette knife and spread the icing with long, smooth strokes over the top and side of the cake. Dip the palette knife in warm water if the icing sticks to it.

FREEZING CAKES

If baked goods are not eaten immediately freezing is a good way to keep them fresh for a long time. Cakes, teabreads, biscuits, American-style muffins, and scones all freeze well.

Wrap plain cakes, fruit cakes, and teabreads in foil or freezer wrap. If a cake has been iced or decorated, tray freeze it, then place in a rigid container or freezer bag. Fruit cake can stored for 4–6 months: iced cakes for 2–3 months. Unwarp decorated cakes before thawing, but leave other cakes in their wrapping.

Biscuits, muffins, and scones can be stored for 6 months. Interleave biscuits with foil or freezer wrap to keep them separate. Thaw biscuits and muffins at room temperature. Scones can be successfully reheated or toasted from frozen.

BEST-EVER BROWNIES

MAKES 24

375g (12oz) plain chocolate,
  broken into pieces
250g (8oz) margarine or butter
2 tsp instant coffee
2 tbsp hot water
2 eggs
250g (8oz) caster sugar
1 tsp vanilla extract
90g (3oz) self-raising flour
175g (6oz) walnut pieces
250g (8oz) plain chocolate chips

1 Grease a 30 × 23cm (12 × 9in) roasting tin, line the base with greaseproof paper, and grease the paper.

2 Put the chocolate and margarine in a bowl and sit the bowl on top of a small saucepan of gently simmering water. Melt the chocolate slowly, then remove the bowl from the pan and let the chocolate cool.

3 Put the coffee in another bowl, pour in the hot water, and stir to dissolve. Add the eggs, sugar, and vanilla essence. Gradually beat in the chocolate mixture. Fold in the flour and walnuts, then the chocolate chips.

4 Pour the mixture into the prepared tin and bake in a preheated oven at 190°C (375°F, Gas 5) for about 40–45 minutes or until firm to the touch. Don't overcook – the crust should be dull and crisp, but the middle may still be gooey. Leave to cool in the tin, then cut into 24 pieces.

left to right: *Chocolate Cup Cakes,*
Best-ever Brownies.

CHOCOLATE CUP CAKES

MAKES 24

2 × 12-HOLE MUFFIN TINS AND 24 PAPER CASES

40g (1¹/₂oz) cocoa powder
about 4 tbsp boiling water
3 eggs
175g (6oz) butter, softened
175g (6oz) caster sugar
115g (4¹/₂oz) self-raising flour
1 rounded tsp baking powder

ICING

60g (2oz) butter
30g (1oz) cocoa powder
about 3 tbsp milk
250g (8oz) icing sugar

1 Line two 12-hole muffin tins with paper cases. Sift the cocoa powder into a bowl, pour in the boiling water, and mix into a thick paste. Add the remaining cake ingredients and mix with an electric hand whisk (or beat well with a wooden spoon).

2 Divide the mixture equally between the 24 paper cases. Bake in a preheated oven at 200°C (400°F, Gas 6) for about 10 minutes until well risen and springy to the touch. Cool in the cases on a wire rack.

3 Make the icing. Melt the butter, then pour it into a bowl. Sift in the cocoa powder and stir to mix. Stir in the milk and then sift in the icing sugar a little at a time to make a glossy, spreadable icing. Spread the icing over the cakes and leave to set before serving.

Illustrated on page 247.

Cocoa lends a rich full flavour to these desserts.

LEMON DRIZZLE CUP CAKES

Substitute the cocoa with the 40g (1½oz) self-raising flour and omit the boiling water. Add finely grated rind of 1 lemon to the basic sponge mix. Mix the juice of 1 lemon with 100g (4oz) granulated sugar and pour over the cup cakes whilst they are still warm and just out of the oven.

CHILDREN'S VANILLA

Substitute the cocoa with the 40g (1½oz) self-raising flour and omit the boiling water. Add 2 tsp of vanilla extract to the sponge mix. For the icing mix together 75g (3oz) sieved icing sugar with a few drops vanilla extract. Decorate the icing with children's favourite sweets eg smarties, jelly babies, 100's and 1000's.

COFFEE AND WALNUT

Substitute the cocoa with the 40g (1½oz) self-raising flour and omit the boiling water. Dissolve 1 tbsp of instant coffee with 2 tsp of water, add to the sponge mix. Stir in 2 tbsp of chopped shelled walnuts. For the icing, mix together, 75g (3oz) sieved icing sugar with 1 tsp of diluted coffee or a few drops of coffee extract.

clockwise from top left: *Lemons with lemon rind, vanilla pods, and walnuts.*

INDEX

Page numbers in *italics* indicate illustrations of recipes.

MARY BERRY

ABOUT THE AUTHOR

Mary Berry is one of the UK's best known and respected cookery writers, a TV cook and Aga expert, and champion of traditional family cooking. With over 60 books to her name, and over 5 million sales worldwide, in 2004 she was voted Top 3 by BBC Good Food for the category "Most Reliable Celebrity Cook Books", alongside Jamie Oliver and Delia Smith.

ACKNOWLEDGMENTS

AUTHOR'S ACKNOWLEDGMENTS FOR *MARY BERRY'S COMPLETE COOKBOOK*

For the first edition, I would like to thank Fiona Oyston for her expertise in writing and testing recipes, and for all her hard work helping me produce the book. I would also like to thank managing editor Gillian Roberts for help in preparing the second edition.

PUBLISHER'S ACKNOWLEDGMENTS FOR *MARY BERRY'S COMPLETE COOKBOOK*

The first (1995) edition of this book was created by Carroll & Brown Ltd for Dorling Kindersley. Thanks to the following people for their help: Editorial consultant, Jeni Wright; Project editor, Vicky Hanson; Editors, Jo-Anne Cox, Stella Vayne, Anne Crane, Sophie Lankenau, and Trish Shine; Cookery consultants, Valerie Cipollone and Anne Hildyard; Art editors, Louise Cameron and Gary Edgar-Hyde; Designers, Alan Watt, Karen Sawyer, and Lucy De Rosa; Photography, David Murray and Jules Selmes, assisted by Nick Allen and Sid Sideris; Production, Wendy Rogers and Amanda Mackie; Food preparation, Eric Treuille, Annie Nichols, Cara Hobday, Sandra Baddeley, and Elaine Ngan, assisted by Maddalena Bastianelli and Sarah Lowman; Additional recipes/Contributors, Marlena Spieler, Sue Ashworth, Louise Pickford, Cara Hobday, Norma MacMillan, and Anne Gains; Nutritional consultant Anne Sheasby.

The second (2003) edition of this book was created by Dorling Kindersley. Thanks to the following people for their help: Editorial contributor, Norma MacMillan; Editorial assistance, Hugh Thompson; DK Picture Library, Claire Bowers and Charlotte Oster; Nutritional consultant, Wendy Doyle; Index, Helen Smith; Loan of props, Villeroy & Boch, Thomas Goode & Co. and Chomett. Thanks also to DK India: Project editor, Dipali Singh; Editor, Kajori Aikat; Project designer, Romi Chakraborty; Designer, Rashmi Battoo; DTP, Narender Kumar, Rajesh Chibber, and Nain Singh Rawat; Managing editor, Ira Pande; Managing art editor, Aparna Sharma.

The publisher would like to thank Susan Bosanko for creating the index and Romaine Werblow for her picture research for *Mary Berry's Traditional Puddings and Desserts*.

The publisher would like to thank the following for their kind permission to reproduce their photographs:

(Key: a-above; b-below/bottom; c-centre; l-left; r-right; t-top)

Jacket images: *Front:* **Rob Judges** and **William Reavell:** tr. *Spine:* **Rob Judges:** t

All other images © Dorling Kindersley
For further information see: www.dkimages.com